A GAP IN THE ENFORCEMENT OF ARTICLE 82

A GAP IN THE ENFORCEMENT OF ARTICLE 82

IOANNIS KOKKORIS

British Institute of
International and
Comparative Law

Published and Distributed by
British Institute of International and Comparative Law
Charles Clore House, 17 Russell Square, London WC1B 5JP

British Library Cataloguing in Publication Data
A Catalogue record of this book is available from the British Library

ISBN 978–1–905221–39–4

Typeset by Cambrian Typesetters
Camberley, Surrey
Printed in Great Britain by the MPG Books Group, Bodmin and King's Lynn

To my family

Contents

Foreword

The application of competition rules to firms' unilateral conduct has been extensively and intensively debated in recent years, making this book very topical. In September 2008, the US Department of Justice published a Report on single-firm conduct under section 2 of the Sherman Act. In December 2008 the European Commission issued guidance on its enforcement priorities in applying Article 82 of the Treaty to abusive exclusionary conduct by dominant undertakings.

The Commission's guidance paper sets out the economic and effects-based approach we take to establishing our enforcement priorities under Article 82. This is in line with the approach we have taken under Article 81 (restrictive business agreements) and mergers since the late 1990s, and indeed in individual cases under Article 82 in recent years. Our work under Article 82 continues, as we are now turning our attention to exploitative conduct by dominant undertakings.

I believe that we now have in place a solid analytical framework for addressing anticompetitive conduct which harms consumers, whether in the form of restrictive business agreements, mergers or abuse of dominance.

Nevertheless, debate is the lifeblood of our competition system. And this book raises interesting questions concerning competition policy, and more specifically the scope of enforcement under Article 82. It also examines the concepts of superior bargaining power and abuse of economic dependence and discusses how some national jurisdictions in the EU have attempted to address these issues.

I am sure that my Commission colleagues and I would strongly agree with Ioannis Kokkoris on some issues and strongly disagree on others. But I very much welcome his lively contribution to this important debate.

Philip Lowe
Director-General
DG Competition—European Commission

Foreword

Ioannis Kokkoris has written a thought-provoking book respecting gaps in the enforcement of Article 82. More specifically, he has accurately identified circumstances in which Article 82 does not apply.

I believe that the law in the United States is not that much different in this respect. For example, he is correct in asserting that the fundamental goal of antitrust law enforcement in the United States is supposed to be the enhancement of consumer welfare. Our Supreme Court said so in *Reiter v Sonotone* 442 US 330 (1979) nearly three decades ago. But since then debate has raged over what is meant by 'consumer welfare'. On the one hand, it may mean (as the book seems to suggest) the welfare of consumers of the output in a market. On the other hand, it may mean (as doctrinaire Chicago School disciples insist) total or societal welfare, which arguably is not enhanced when practices by firms that are not 'dominant' are challenged. Similarly, the United States Supreme Court long ago declared in *Copperweld Corp v Independence Tube Corp* 467 US 752 (1984) that single firm conduct of the sort condemned in section 2 of the Sherman Act (and Article 82) is less pernicious than concerted conduct that is the subject of section 1 of the Sherman Act (and Article 81), and the Court has since held in *Spectrum Sprts v McQuillan* 506 US 447 (1993) that all section 2 challenges must demonstrate that the defendant has such substantial market power that its practices pose a dangerous probability that it will achieve monopoly power. Those cases suggest that generally a practice by a single firm lacking dominance in its market is not subject to challenge in the United States. (To be sure, that is not true of a challenge under the Robinson-Patman Act, which prohibits discriminatory practices under certain circumstances, but that Act is much-criticized and under heavy assault.)

Additionally, as it is argued in the book, it is not clear that the EC would consider the circumstances identified in the book as 'gaps' in the enforcement of Article 82. The recent Article 82 Guidance issued by the EC describes a 'soft' safe harbor under which a firm must have at least a 40 per cent market share in order to be considered dominant under Article 82, and the central thesis of that Guidance is that practices truly threaten consumer welfare only when they are undertaken in circumstances in which competition will be so crippled that rivals will not be able to constrain an exercise of monopoly or at least near monopoly power. These features of the Guidance seem to imply that the practices of a firm which is not dominant in its market should be of no concern under Article 82 or otherwise.

This book creates food for thought about all of these controversial matters.

Commissioner Tom Rosch
Federal Trade Commission, Washington DC, USA

Preface

The EC has acknowledged and respected, in Regulation 1/2003, the ability of the Member States to apply stricter rules than Article 82.

There are two types of conduct that cannot be addressed by Article 82 because the undertakings involved are not dominant. One relates to conduct by non-dominant firms against other firms in weaker bargaining positions. The concepts of superior dominant bargaining position and abuse of economic dependence, typically include the conduct of undertakings which are able to exercise market power only to a certain extent and in relation to certain undertakings which are deemed to be capable of having negative effects on competition. In some EU jurisdictions the concept applies to non-dominant undertakings with relative market power in relation to small and medium-sized suppliers or purchasers, and to non-dominant undertakings with superior market power in relation to small and medium-sized competitors. In other EU jurisdictions the scope of application of this concept is narrower and applies to the retail sector or only to the buyer side of the market.

The concept of abuse of superior bargaining position is a concept which is incorporated into the legislation of some Member States but is not in the EC legislation. This omission results in anti-competitive conduct not being caught by the European Commission. Non-dominant firms can adopt conduct that may lead to harmful foreclosure and to consumer harm.

The second type of conduct relates to the anti-competitive conduct that non-dominant firms may adopt towards consumers (eg price discrimination, excessive pricing). Abuse of economic dependence relates to conduct by non-dominant firms, which induce significant harm to consumers. Article 82 is not applicable to firms that are not dominant, but as this book will illustrate, there are instances where non-dominant firms have the ability to behave independently of customers and competitors and adopt conduct which will induce consumer harm. Such conduct cannot be addressed though under Article 82. This gap in the application of Article 82 arises in all situations that the two biggest firms have close and significant market shares, their products are differentiated and although the biggest firm's conduct would be considered abusive, the second biggest would not. In addition, it may arise when the rivals of the non-dominant undertaking in a homogeneous market face capacity constraints, and thus cannot react to anti-competitive conduct adopted by the non-dominant firm.

Such conduct is not caught by the abuse of superior bargaining position and abuse of economic dependence legislation that some jurisdictions have enacted. If the two latter concepts apply only to the retail sector (eg Ireland) or only to the buyer side of the market (eg Latvia, Slovak Republic, Czech

Republic), or only to conduct against firms, they do not encompass all the possible anti-competitive conduct that the non-dominant firm can adopt. Thus, in such jurisdictions non-dominant firms can induce consumer harm.

It should be emphasized that Article 82 would not apply at all to the anti-competitive conduct that non-dominant firms may adopt towards consumers. Thus, non-dominant firms can price-discriminate or price excessively, inducing consumer harm, since Article 82 will not be applicable at all to such conduct. Taking into account that there is a trend towards an effects-based approach in Article 82 cases, focusing on consumer welfare, the fact that there is conduct that induces consumer harm and cannot be addressed by Article 82 is surprising and worrying.

As we will see in this book, the UK and the USA can address conduct of non-dominant firms by enforcing specific legislation which will be analysed herein. Some EU jurisdictions apply the concept of abuse of superior dominant bargaining position/abuse of economic dependence in order to address anti-competitive conduct of non-dominant firms. The scope of application differs amongst these countries (eg only on buyer side, grocery sector).

The Commission cannot address anti-competitive conduct of non-dominant firms which induce significant consumer harm. This has resulted from the application of the dominance concept and from the dependence of a finding of a dominant firm on the market share of the firm. As the analysis herein will illustrate, applying the concept of dominance in that way means that a non-dominant firm in a differentiated market can adopt anti-competitive conduct and not be deterred by the possible application of Article 82.

The research for this book has been conducted during my post-doctorate research at Harvard Law School (USA) and my employment as a Consultant at the Federal Trade Commission (USA).

The author has benefited from discussions with John Fingleton (Office of Fair Trading); Einer Elhauge (Harvard Law School); Philip Marsden (British Institute of International Comparative Law); Kenneth Glazer (Federal Trade Commission); Randolph Tritell (Federal Trade Commission); Francisco DeMiranda (Federal Trade Commission); Alden Abbott (Federal Trade Commission); Greg Werden (Department of Justice); Luc Peppercorn (European Commission, DG Competition); Markus Lange (Bundeskartellamt); and Etienne Pfister (Conseil de la Concurrence). I am very grateful for their comments and should emphasize that any errors herein are the sole responsibility of the author.

I owe my gratitude to Philip Marsden for his invaluable guidance in this book. Finally, I would like to especially thank Orla Fee, for her commitment to this work.

Dr Ioannis Kokkoris
London, November 2008

Introduction

The Treaty of Rome 1957 provides for Regulations or Directives to be made to determine the relationship between national laws and Articles 81 EC Treaty ('Article 81') and 82 EC Treaty ('Article 82').[1] Article 3 of Regulation 1/2003 is the first such measure.

According to Article 3(2) of Regulation 1/2003:

> 'The application of national competition law may not lead to the prohibition of agreements, decisions by associations of undertakings or concerted practices which may affect trade between Member States but which do not restrict competition within the meaning of Article 81(1) of the Treaty, or which fulfil the conditions of Article 81(3) of the Treaty or which are covered by a Regulation for the application of Article 81(3) of the Treaty. Member States shall not under this Regulation be precluded from adopting and applying on their territory stricter national laws which prohibit or sanction unilateral conduct engaged in by undertakings.'

As regards the relationship between Article 82 and national law, Article 3 of Regulation 1/2003 does not compromise the application of specific national law provisions permitting Member States to address specific issues with which EC law could not deal appropriately. Article 3(2) does not specify expressly Article 82 as the comparator for the 'stricter' national law and it does not refer to dominance. Recital 8 gives as an illustration of stricter national laws prohibiting unilateral conduct.

According to Recital 8:

> '... Member States should not under this Regulation be precluded from adopting and applying on their territory stricter national competition laws which prohibit or impose sanctions on unilateral conduct engaged in by undertakings. These stricter national laws may include provisions which prohibit or impose sanctions on abusive behaviour toward economically dependent undertakings. Furthermore, this Regulation does not apply to national laws which impose criminal sanctions on natural persons except to the extent that such sanctions are the means whereby competition rules applying to undertakings are enforced.'

In addition, according to According to Recital 9:

[1] Article 83(2).

'(9) ... Member States may under this Regulation implement on their territory national legislation that prohibits or imposes sanctions on acts of unfair trading practice, be they unilateral or contractual. Such legislation pursues a specific objective, irrespective of the actual or presumed effects of such acts on competition on the market. This is particularly the case of legislation which prohibits undertakings from imposing on their trading partners, obtaining or attempting to obtain from them terms and conditions that are unjustified, disproportionate or without consideration.'

Thus, the European Commission ('Commission') has acknowledged and respected, in Regulation 1/2003, the ability of the Member States to apply stricter rules than Article 82. These national laws in some EU jurisdictions tackle the abuse of economic dependence. Abuse of economic dependence relates to conduct by non-dominant firms, which induces significant harm to consumers.

Article 82 is not applicable to firms that are not dominant, but as this book will illustrate, there are instances where non-dominant firms have the ability to behave independently of customers and competitors and adopt conduct which will induce consumer harm. Such conduct cannot, however, be addressed under Article 82. This gap in the application of Article 82 arises in all situations that the two biggest firms have close market shares, their products are differentiated and although the biggest firm's conduct would be considered abusive, the second biggest[2] would not.

As the analysis herein will illustrate, there are two types of conduct that cannot be addressed by Article 82 because the undertakings involved are not dominant. One relates to conduct by non-dominant firms against other firms in weaker bargaining positions. The concept of superior bargaining position/abuse of economic dependence[3] typically includes conduct of undertakings able to exercise market power only to a certain extent and in relation to certain undertakings which are deemed to be capable of having negative effects on competition. In some EU jurisdictions the concept applies to non-dominant undertakings with relative market power in relation to small and medium-sized suppliers or purchasers, and to non-dominant undertakings with superior market power in relation to small and medium-sized competitors.[4] In other EU jurisdictions the scope of applica-

[2] Although throughout this book, reference will be made to the second biggest firm in the market, the same arguments can be made for the firms with similar market shares in a differentiated products market. Thus, if the third biggest firm's market share is similar to the top two, the same arguments as regards the consumer harm induced by adopting possible anti-competitive conduct can be made.

[3] The two terms will be used interchangeably.

[4] Examples of conduct that constitutes abuse of superior bargaining position in Germany

tion of this concept is narrower and applies to the retail sector or only the buyer side of the market.[5]

However, this concept is not addressed at all in Article 82. The latter fact, as we will see, allows non-dominant firms to adopt conduct that may lead to harmful foreclosure and to consumer harm. The International Competition Network has identified the importance of the abuse of superior bargaining position and initiated a working group on this concept which presented its findings in the International Competition Network ('ICN') annual conference in Kyoto in April 2008.

The second type of conduct relates to the anti-competitive conduct that non-dominant firms may adopt towards consumers (eg price discrimination, excessive pricing). Such conduct is not caught by the abuse of economic dependence legislation in some of the jurisdictions. If the concept applies only to the retail sector (eg Ireland) or only to the buyer side of the market (eg Latvia, Slovak Republic, Czech Republic), or only to conduct against firms, it does not encompass all the possible anti-competitive conduct that the non-dominant firm can adopt. Thus, in jurisdictions applying such legislation, non-dominant firms can induce consumer harm. In particular, UK and the USA can address a wider range of anti-competitive conduct by non-dominant firms by enforcing specific legislation which will be analysed herein.

It should be emphasized that Article 82 would not apply at all to the anti-competitive conduct that non-dominant firms may adopt towards consumers. Thus, non-dominant firms can price-discriminate or price excessively, inducing consumer harm, since Article 82 will not be applicable at all to such conduct. Taking into account that there is a trend towards an effects-based approach in Article 82 cases, focusing on consumer welfare, the fact that there are sorts of conduct that induce consumer harm and cannot be addressed by Article 82 is surprising and worrying.

This book will address in detail these two situations where non-dominant firms adopt conduct which induces consumer harm and cannot be caught by Article 82. After presenting an analysis of the objective of Article

(one of the countries which have enacted legislation against such conduct) include demanding retrospective rebates, refusal to supply undertakings with 'must-stock' items, abusive and unjustified setting of sales prices by a franchisor, agreements on an exclusive purchasing obligation within a franchising system purchasing benefits are not passed on to the franchisee, manufacturers requiring trading firms to comply with their provisions in terms of quantities and turnovers on the type of resale; eg the setting of a maximum threshold for internet sales without any objective justification, deliberate non-disclosure of interface information in the software sector by a car manufacturer. See further: Seventh Annual Conference of the International Competition Network, Special Program on Abuse of Superior Bargaining Position, Germany response. http://www.icn-kyoto.org/documents/germany.pdf. ('ICN Kyoto-ASBP').

[5] Other jurisdictions (eg US, UK) consider such issues to be contract rather then competition related.

82, the book will briefly address the concept of dominance and then it will analyse in detail the concept of superior bargaining position/abuse of economic dependence and will illustrate the gaps in the application of Article 82. Before presenting some concluding thoughts, the book will attempt to propose means to rectify the gap in the enforcement of Article 82.

CHAPTER 1

Objectives of Article 82

Turning briefly to the objectives of Article 82, in the EU the notion of harm to consumers should hence be read in conjunction with that of harm to the process of competition, although the two notions are quite distinct. Moreover, consumer welfare is an aim which should be viewed dynamically, ie by examining also its dimensions on a mid- and long-term basis.[1] Article 82 prohibits an abuse of a dominant position within the common market or in a substantial part of it. The concern of the EC competition rules is therefore to prevent conduct by a dominant undertaking which risks weakening competition still further, and harming consumers.[2]

In contrast to American antitrust law, there has been continuing debate over the concept of consumer welfare referring to a narrower or broader meaning. There are three components of consumer welfare.[3] The first component is value for money. Consumer welfare is enhanced if the price of goods/services is reduced or the quality of those goods is increased while the price is not changed. Price and quality are connected where a price means the sum payable for goods/services of a particular quality. However, a consumer is not interested in the quality of goods/services unless the consumer also knows their price. Quality is important because if prices in a market reach marginal costs, this may lead to a switch from higher quality to lower quality goods/services; indeed, this situation depends on the consumers and their sensitivity to price. The second component is consumer choice. Choice does not have value in itself. Nonetheless, if consumers have

[1] V Mertikopoulou, 'DG Competition's discussion paper on the application of Article 82 of the EC Treaty to exclusionary abuses: the proposed economic reform from a legal point of view' [2007] 28 (4) ECLR 241–251, 242. In competition law the primary role of the consumer welfare standard is to verify the goals of competition policy and to delineate the general legal framework of competition law enforcement by establishing the basis for the standard of proof required in investigation and litigation.

[2] The Economic Advisory Group for Competition Policy in its report on Article 82 argued that the use of the single term 'consumer welfare' conceals the fact that it refers to a multi-facetted concern. Many issues concern multiple markets, with consumer welfare effects going in different directions in the different markets. The competition authority needs to take a comprehensive view, taking account of the different effects of the practices under investigation and of policy interventions on consumer welfare. See further Report by the EAGCP—'*An economic approach to Article 82*', 9. http://ec.europa.eu/comm/competition/antitrust/art82/index.html. ('EAGCP Report').

[3] A Lindsay, *The EC Merger Regulation: Substantive Issues* (Sweet & Maxwell, London, 2003).

different tastes, then consumer welfare may increase if they can choose from a wider variation of products. The last component is innovation. Consumers may benefit and consumer welfare may increase if new products/services are developed, on the basis that there is actual or potential demand for the new products/services.[4]

Promotion of consumer welfare has traditionally been considered as one of the aims, not the sole aim, of antitrust, both in the United States and in Europe.[5] In the United States the Federal Trade Commission ('FTC') acts to ensure that markets operate efficiently to benefit *consumers*. In the UK the Office of Fair Trading ('OFT') declares that the OFT's goal is to make markets work well *for consumers*. Most academics seem to agree that consumer protection is the prevailing aim of antitrust legislation.[6]

Early European Commission ('Commission') Reports on Competition Policy strongly suggested that European competition policy was aimed at the promotion of consumer welfare. The European Commission's First Report on competition policy in 1971, stated that:

> '[C]ompetition policy endeavours to maintain or create effective conditions of competition by means of rules applying to enterprises in both private and public sectors. Such a policy encourages the best possible use of productive resources for the greatest possible benefit of the economy as a whole and for the benefit, in particular of the consumer'.

The Commission and the European Court of Justice ('ECJ') in their fundamental decisions reached in the 1970s interpreted the objective of protecting competition as referring to the protection of the economic freedom of market actors. These important decisions were not based on economics or consumer welfare. In these early cases the Commission and Community courts were not focused on consumer welfare, but on the protection of the

[4] J Malinauskaite, 'The development of "consumer welfare" and its application in the competition law of the European Community and Lithuania' [2007] 18(10) ICCLR 354–364, 355.

[5] R Whish, *Competition Law* (5th edn, Butterworths, UK, 2003) 15 f.

[6] Annex 1 presents a table (taken from the ICN Report) of the objectives of unilateral conduct laws identified in the responses of the jurisdictions which were surveyed as part of the ICN Report. The report prepared by the ICN Unilateral Conduct Working Group (ICN Report) for the 6th Annual Conference of the ICN in May 2007 in Moscow consists of three chapters, which address: 1) the Objectives of Unilateral Conduct Laws; 2) the Assessment of Dominance/Substantial Market Power; and 3) State-Created Monopolies. The report describes the approaches of competition agencies around the world to these issues, and distills themes that may assist in promoting convergence in these areas. The report is based on the responses of ICN Members and non-governmental advisors (NGAs) to a questionnaire developed by the working group http://www.internationalcompetitionnetwork.org/media/library/unilateral_conduct/Objectives%20of%20Unilateral%20Conduct%20May%2007.pdf.

economic freedom of the market players as well as on preventing firms from using their economic power to undermine competitive structures.[7]

In *Continental Can*, the Court ruled:

> '... abuse may therefore occur if an undertaking in a dominant position strengthens such position in such a way that the degree of dominance reached substantially fetters competition, i.e. that only undertakings remain in the market whose behaviour depends on the dominant one ... it can ... be regarded as an abuse if an undertaking holds a position so dominant that the objectives of the Treaty are circumvented by an alteration to the supply structure which seriously endangers the consumer's freedom of action in the market such a case necessarily exists if practically all competition is eliminated.'[8]

The ECJ in that case concluded that Article 82 is aimed at practices which may cause damage to consumers directly, as well as at practices that are detrimental to consumers through their impact on an effective competitive structure.[9]

Advocate General Jacobs has stated that:[10]

> '[I]t is important not to lose sight of the fact that the primary purpose of article 82 is to prevent distortion of competition—and in particular to safeguard the interest of consumers—rather than to protect the position of particular competitors.'

The Court of First Instance ('CFI') in the *British Airways* case explained:

> 'Article 82 EC does not require it to be demonstrated that the conduct in question had any actual or direct effect on consumers. Competition law concentrates upon protecting the market structure from artificial distortions because by doing so the interests of the consumer in the medium to long term are best protected.'[11]

[7] L Gormsen, 'Article 82 EC: Where are we coming from and where are we going to?', The Competition Law Review, vol 2, issue 2, March 2006, 19.

[8] Case 6/72 *Europemballage Corp and Continental Can Co Inc v Commission* (Continental Can) [1973] ECR I-215, § 26.

[9] See also the Opinion of AG Kokott in *BA v Commission* (*British Airways Plc v Commission*, C95/04 P) § 69, about the protective purpose of Article 82 being to protect the structure of the market and thus competition as such because where competition as such is damaged, disadvantages for the consumers are also to be feared.

[10] Opinion in the Oscar Bronner case 231 (*Oscar Bronner v Mediaprint* C-7/97 [1998] ECR I-7791).

[11] *British Airways v Commission* 264.

The European Commission Notice on the Application of Article 81(3) provides that:

> 'The concept of "consumers" encompasses all direct or indirect users of the products covered by the agreement, including producers that use the products as an input, wholesalers, retailers and final consumers, i.e. natural persons who are acting for purposes which can be regarded as outside their trade or profession. In other words, consumers within the meaning of Article 81(3) are the customers of the parties to the agreement and subsequent purchasers. These customers can be undertakings as in the case of buyers of industrial machinery or an input for further processing or final consumers as for instance in the case of buyers of impulse ice-cream or bicycles.'[12]

The Commission further states that[13] the objective of Article 81 is to protect competition on the market as a means of enhancing consumer welfare, which must be the same for Article 82 as Article 81 and 82 seek to achieve the same aim.[14]

Commissioner Kroes argued that:

> '[C]onsumer welfare is now well established as the standard the Commission applies when assessing mergers and infringements of the Treaty rules on cartels and monopolies ... An effects-based approach, grounded in solid economics, ensures that citizens enjoy the benefits of a competitive, dynamic market economy.'[15]

In addition, Commissioner Kroes in her speech of 23 September 2005 to the Fordham Corporate Law Institute mentioned that *the objective of Article 82 is the protection of competition on the market as a means of enhancing consumer welfare and ensuring an efficient allocation of resources.*[16]

[12] *European Commission Notice Guidelines on the Application of Article 81(3)* [2004] OJ C101, para 84.

[13] *European Commission Notice Guidelines on the Application of Article 81(3)* [2004] OJ C101, paragraphs 13 and 33.

[14] Case C-6/72 *Continental Can v Commission* [1973] ECR 215, § 25.

[15] N Kroes, '*European Competition Policy: Delivering Better Markets and Better Choices*', 15 September 2005, available at http://europa.eu/rapid/pressReleasesAction.do?reference=SPEECH/05/512 &format=HTML&aged=0&language=EN&guiLanguage =en.

[16] N Kroes, '*Preliminary Thoughts on Policy Review of Article 82*' speech given on 23 September at the Fordham Corporate Law Institute New York (2005). http://europa.eu/rapid/pressReleasesAction.do?reference=SPEECH/05/537&format=HTML&aged=0&language=EN&guiLanguage=en.

Director General of DG Competition, Philip Lowe emphasized that 'competition is not an end in itself, but an instrument designed to achieve a certain public interest objective, consumer welfare'.[17]

According to Eilmansberger,[18] the objective of Article 82 is ultimately pursued for the benefit of consumer and consumer welfare is one, if not the foremost rationale of abuse control. Article 82 applies to practices that directly and indirectly[19] damage consumers.

The Economic Advisory Group for Competition Policy in its report on Article 82 states that:

> Referring to this [consumer welfare added] standard is all the more important because, in the actual proceedings on a given case, competitors are usually much better organized than consumers. The competition authority receives more complaints and more material from competitors, so the procedure tends to be biased towards the protection of competitors. Developing a routine for assessing consumer welfare effects provides a counterweight to this bias.[20]

The Economic Advisory Group adds that an economic approach to Article 82 focuses on improved consumer welfare and thus avoids confusing the protection of competition with the protection of competitors. An economics-based approach requires a careful examination of how competition works in each particular market in order to evaluate how specific company strategies affect consumer welfare. Such an approach ensures that anti-competitive behaviour does not outwit legal provisions and guarantees that the statutory provisions do not unduly thwart pro-competitive strategies.[21]

According to the *Guidance on the Commission's Enforcement Priorities in Applying Article 82 EC Treaty to Abusive Exclusionary Conduct by Dominant Undertakings* ('Guidance Paper'):[22]

[17] 'Preserving and Promoting Competition: A European Response', EC Competition Policy Newsletter, 2006–Number 2–Summer.

[18] Eilsmanberger T (2006), 'Dominance—The Lost Child? How Effects Based Rules Could and Should Change Analysis', European Competition Journal 15–29, 18.

[19] Through their impact on the structure of competition. See further: T Eilsmanberger (n 18) 15–29, 18, for a list of relevant cases.

[20] Report by the EAGCP, 'An Economic Approach to Article 82' (July 2005) 9.

[21] See further page 2. EAGCP Report.

[22] http://ec.europa.eu/comm/competition/antitrust/art82/ guidance_en.pdf. For comments on the Discussion Paper see indicatively Niels/Jenkins, 'Reform of Article 82: Where the Link Between Dominance and Effects Breaks Down' [2005] ECLR 605; Bishop/Marsden, Editorial, 'The Article 82 Discussion Paper: A missed opportunity' [2006] European Competition Journal 1; D S Evans & A J Padilla, 'Designing Antitrust Rules for Assessing Unilateral Practices: A Neo-Chicago Approach' 72 U Chi L Rev 73, 90–91 (2005); J Tirole, 'The Analysis of Tying Cases: A Primer' [2005] 1 Comp Policy Int'l 14–15; R O'Donoghue and A J Padilla, *The Law and Economics of Article 82 EC* (2006) 482.

> In applying Article 82 to exclusionary conduct by dominant undertakings, the Commission will focus on those types of conduct that are most harmful to consumers. ... The Commission, therefore, will direct its enforcement to ensuring that markets function properly and that consumers benefit from the efficiency and productivity which result from effective competition betwen undertakings.
>
> 'The central concern of Article 82 with regard to exclusionary abuses is thus foreclosure that hinders competition and thereby harms consumers.'[23]

The Guidance paper seems to adopt an approach, advocating that an anti-competitive conduct is not prohibited unless it entails significant consumer harm, after an off-setting of the harm to consumers against the (mainly short-term) benefits for the consumers has been effected.[24]

Consumer harm is the overall criterion for deciding whether a dominant firm's behaviour is abusive or not. According to Fjell and Sorgard, the discussion paper proposes an effects approach, implying that the appropriate test for abuse would be to check whether consumers are harmed.[25]

According to Cseres:

> '[T]he adoption of the consumer welfare standard vis-à-vis the total welfare standard places consumers' economic needs and responses to firm behaviour further into the focus of competition law enforcement. It, counterbalances firms' information advantages, lobbying advantages, the fact they are better represented, as well as their first mover advantages in selecting the strategic moves they pursue. The consumer welfare standard seems, from both the legal and political aspect, an appropriate standard of enforcement.'[26]

[23] § 56.

[24] See also EAGCP Report, http://ec.europa.eu/comm/competition/publications/studies/eagcp july 21 05.pdf. As stated therein: 'An economics-based approach to the application of article 82 implies that the assessment of each specific case will not be undertaken on the basis of the form that a particular business practice takes (for example, exclusive dealing, tying, etc.) but rather will be based on the assessment of the anti-competitive effects generated by business behaviour. This implies that competition authorities will need to identify a competitive harm, and assess the extent to which such a negative effect on consumers is potentially outweighed by efficiency gains. The identification of competitive harm requires spelling out a consistent business behaviour based on sound economics and supported by facts and empirical evidence. Similarly, efficiencies and how they are passed on to consumers should be properly justified on the basis of economic analysis and grounded on the facts of each case.'

[25] K Fjel, L Sorgard (2006), 'How to Test for Abuse of Dominance' [2006] European Competition Journal, July, 69.

[26] K J Cseres, 'The Controversies of the Consumer Welfare Standard' [2007] Competition Law Review, vol 3 issue 2, 170.

Virtually all[27] responding agencies to a report on unilateral conduct prepared by the ICN argued that ensuring an effective competitive process is an objective in its own right, a means to achieve other desirable goals such as consumer welfare, economic freedom or efficiency, or both an objective and a means to achieve such goals. Of the nine other objectives that respondents identified as objectives in and of themselves, a significant number[28] of respondents relied on the promotion of consumer welfare and maximizing efficiency.[29]

The *Microsoft*[30] case is contrary to the trend that the Commission seems to be following in the Guidance Paper towards a consumer welfare objective in Article 82 cases. In this case, the CFI upheld an allegation of an abuse, made by the Commission which did not focus on consumer harm since no such harm was evident from that abuse. In order to address the implications of this case on the objective of Article 82, a brief background of the case is necessary.[31]

The Commission identified three separate product markets, namely the markets for, client PC operating systems, work group server operating systems and streaming media players. All markets were of a worldwide dimension.

According to the Commission, Microsoft Corporation infringed Article 82 by:

—refusing to supply interoperability information and allow its use for the purpose of developing and distributing work group server operating system products;
—making the availability of the Windows Client PC Operating System conditional on the simultaneous acquisition of Windows Media Player (WMP).

As regards the refusal to supply, Microsoft had refused to provide Sun with information enabling it to design work group server operating systems that could seamlessly integrate into the 'Active Directory domain architecture', a web of interrelated client PC-to-server and server-to-server protocols that organize Windows work group networks. Microsoft's refusal risked eliminating competition in the relevant market for work group server operating systems because the refused input was

27 32 agencies.

28 30 agencies.

29 See further ICN Report, 5. See also Annex 1 of this book.

30 *Microsoft* [2007] OJ L 32/23, *Microsoft Corp v Commission*, T-201/04 R, [2004] ECR II-4463, *Microsoft Corp v Commission* T-201/04, 17/09/2007.

31 See I Kokkoris, *Competition Cases from the European Union* (Sweet and Maxwell, London, 2007).

indispensable for competitors operating in that market. Microsoft's refusal limited technical development to the prejudice of consumers, in contradiction in particular to Article 82(b). If competitors had access to the refused information, they would be able to provide new and enhanced products to consumers. The Commission further considered that Microsoft's refusal to Sun was part of a general pattern of conduct. It also asserted that Microsoft's conduct involved a disruption of previous, higher levels of supply, and caused a risk of elimination of competition on the work group server operating systems.

As regards tying, the Commission argued that Microsoft infringed Article 82 by tying WMP with the Windows PC operating system (Windows). The Commission based its finding of a tying abuse on four elements: (i) Microsoft held a dominant position in the PC operating system market; (ii) the Windows PC operating system and WMP were two separate products; (iii) Microsoft did not give customers a choice to obtain Windows without WMP; and (iv) this tying foreclosed competition. In addition, the Commission rejected Microsoft's arguments to justify the tying of WMP. The Commission argued that the tying of WMP to Windows foreclosed competition and afforded Microsoft unmatched ubiquity of its media player on PCs worldwide.

The CFI argued that the refusal by an undertaking holding a dominant position to license a third party to use a product covered by an intellectual property right could not in itself constitute an abuse of a dominant position within the meaning of Article 82. It was only in exceptional circumstances that the exercise of the exclusive right by the owner of the intellectual property right might give rise to such an abuse. It added that the following circumstances, in particular, must be considered to be exceptional:

- in the first place, the refusal relates to a product or service indispensable to the exercise of a particular activity on a neighbouring market;
- in the second place, the refusal is of such a kind as to exclude any effective competition on that neighbouring market;
- in the third place, the refusal prevents the appearance of a new product for which there is potential consumer demand.

Once it is established that such circumstances are present, the refusal by the holder of a dominant position to grant a licence may infringe Article 82 unless the refusal is objectively justified. Microsoft did not prove that these circumstances were not present and there was no objective justification.

The CFI concluded that the Commission analysis of bundling was correct. The Commission argued that Microsoft had a dominant position on the client PC operating systems market. The Commission added that streaming media players and client PC operating systems are two separate products. In addition, the Commission stated that Microsoft did not give customers the choice of obtaining Windows without Windows Media Player and that the tying of Windows Media Player forecloses competition in the media players market, and cannot be objectively justified. The CFI argued that the Commission was correct to find that client PC operating systems and streaming media players constituted separate products.

It further argued that as regards the abusive refusal to supply, the Commission took issue with Microsoft for having used, by leveraging, its quasi-monopoly on the client PC operating systems market to influence the work group server operating systems market. In other words, Microsoft's abusive conduct had its origin in its dominant position on the first product market. Even if the Commission were wrongly to have considered that Microsoft was in a dominant position on the second market, that could not therefore of itself suffice to support a finding that the Commission was wrong to conclude that there had been an abuse of a dominant position by Microsoft.

The decision of the CFI is somewhat surprising, since it upheld both infringements, although the Windows Media Player did not seem to induce consumer demand as a standalone product. Thus, there seemed to be no actual consumer harm from bundling the Media Player with Windows. This per se type approach contradicts the rule of reason approach that the Commission seems to envisage using in Article 82 cases.[32]

It will be interesting to see how the Commission will reconcile the thinking of the CFI in its *Microsoft* judgment with the general trend towards an effects-based approach in Article 82 cases. The decision of the CFI came as a shock to the legal community as it was expected that the CFI would not uphold the Commission's arguments on the bundling abuse due to the lack of consumer harm. It will be a step backwards in the development of the competition case law if the trend towards consumer welfare objective in Article 82 cases is diverted as a result of the *Microsoft* judgment.

Following the Discussion paper, the Commission issued guidelines on the enforcement priorities in Article 82 cases in an attempt to clarify its approach in the enforcement of Article 82. The enforcement guidelines are less 'radical' compared to the approach when reform of Article 82 was raised in the Discussion Paper. The guidelines seek to distinguish between competition on the merits, which has beneficial effects for consumers and should therefore be promoted and competition that is liable to lead to harmful foreclosure. The assessment of market power will be dependent on the dynamics of the market and the extent to which products are differentiated. A 'soft'

[32] Evidence on the Commission's Enforcement Priorities in Applying Article 82 EC Treaty to Abusive Exclusionary Conduct by Dominant Undertakings. http://ec.europa.eu/competition/antitrust/art82/guidance/pdf.

safe harbour of 40 per cent market share is established. The Commission will also consider barriers to entry and countervailing buyer power. The Commission will only penalixe conduct that is likely to harm competition and ultimately consumers rather than conducts that are likely to harm competitors. The Commission will examine direct evidence of any exclusionary strategy, including internal documents which may be helpful to interpret the dominant company's conduct. In assessing a potentially abusive pricing conduct, the Commission will intervene if the behaviour excludes or impedes an 'as efficient' competitor. A dominant firm will be able to rely on an 'efficiency' defence, if conduct generates 'efficiencies' so that there is a net benefit to consumers. The burden of proof is on the dominant company.

CHAPTER 2

Concept of Dominance

The European Union has its origins in the common market established by the European Coal and Steel Treaty in 1952.[1] The aim of the ECSC Treaty, as stated in Article 2, was to contribute, through the common market for coal and steel, to economic expansion, growth of employment and a rising standard of living. In the light of the establishment of the common market, the ECSC Treaty introduced the free movement of products without customs duties or taxes. It prohibited discriminatory measures or practices, subsidies, aids granted by States or special charges imposed by States and restrictive practices. The Treaty dealt specifically with three elements which could distort competition: agreements,[2] concentrations and the abuse of dominant position.

Article 66(7) of the ECSC Treaty was based on dominance.[3] The origins of the notion of dominance can be traced back to German competition law. The German competition law (*Gesetz gegen Wettbewerbsbeschränkungen* ('GWB')[4]) used the term 'dominance' in section 22(1); it was a familiar concept due to the previous Abuse Regulation of 1923.[5] One reason for adopting the term dominance rather than the term monopolization which

[1] The ECSC Treaty expired on 23 July 2002. Thus, the coal and steel sectors are now subject to Articles 81 and 82, rather than Articles 65 and 66 ECSC. The consequences of this expiry are explained in the Commission's document Communication from the Commission concerning certain aspects of the treatment of competition cases resulting from the expiry of the ECSC Treaty OJ [2002] C152/5, [2002] 5 CMLR 1036, Section 2: http://europa.eu.int/eur-lex/pri/en/oj/dat/2002/c_152/c_15220020626en 00050012.pdf.

[2] Agreements or associations between undertakings could be cancelled by the High Authority if they directly or indirectly prevented, restricted or distorted normal competition.

[3] Article 66(7) was concerned with the concept of a dominant position: If the High Authority finds that public or private undertakings which, in law or in fact, hold or acquire in the market for one of the products within its jurisdiction a dominant position shielding them against effective competition in a substantial part of the common market are using that position for purposes contrary to the objectives of this Treaty, it shall make to them such recommendations as may be appropriate to prevent the position from being so used. If these recommendations are not implemented satisfactorily within a reasonable time, the High Authority shall, by decisions taken in consultation with the Government concerned, determine the prices and conditions of sale to be applied by the undertaking in question or draw up production or delivery programmes with which it must comply, subject to liability to the penalties provided for in Articles 58, 59 and 64.

[4] Available from the Bundeskartellamt website http://www.bundeskartellamt.de/wDeutsch/index.shtml ?navid=27.

[5] Verordnung Gegen Missbrauch Wirtschaftlicher Machtstellungen, 1923, Reichsbesetzblatt, [R6B.1] I, 1067, 2 November 1923.

is used in the Sherman Act[6] is the influence that the German competition law had on the drafter of the ECSC Treaty, Jean Monnet.

The notion of dominance has been addressed both in law and economics. In the realm of economics, dominance has been addressed by theories dealing with oligopolistic and monopolistic market structures. In the realm of law, the concept of dominance is found in two sets of legal provisions, namely Article 82[7] and the ECMR.[8] The legal definition of dominance has been an issue of intense debate. The standard legal definition of dominance was laid down by the ECJ in *United Brands*.

The ECJ stated that:

> The dominant position thus referred to (by Article [82]) relates to a position of economic strength enjoyed by an undertaking which enables it to prevent effective competition being maintained on the relevant market by affording it the power to behave to an appreciable extent independently of its competitors, customers and ultimately of its consumers.[9]

In *Hoffmann-La Roche*[10] the ECJ defined the notion of dominance as 'a position of economic strength enjoyed by an undertaking, which enables it to behave to an appreciable extent independently of its competitors, its customers and ultimately of consumers'.

The ECJ further stated in *Hoffman-La Roche*:

> Furthermore although the importance of the market shares may vary from one market to another the view may legitimately be taken that very large shares are in themselves, and save in exceptional circumstances, evidence of the existence of a dominant position. An undertaking which has a very large market share and holds it for some time (...) is by virtue of that share in a position of strength...[11]

[6] 15 USC §2: Monopolizing trade a felony; penalty
Every person who shall monopolize, or attempt to monopolize, or combine or conspire with any other person or persons, to monopolize any part of the trade or commerce among the several States, or with foreign nations, shall be deemed guilty of a felony, and, on conviction thereof, shall be punished by fine not exceeding $10,000,000 if a corporation, or, if any other person, $350,000, or by imprisonment not exceeding three years, or by both said punishments, in the discretion of the court.

[7] Articles 81 and 82 of the EC Treaty (ex 85 and 86 prior to the Treaty of Amsterdam which came into force on 1 May 1999. Article 12 of the Treaty of Amsterdam provided for the renumbering of the EC Treaty Articles). The EC Treaty was signed on 25 March 1957.

[8] Article 82 deals with the abuse of an already existing dominant position (ex post), whereas the ECMR deals with the prospective assessment of dominance (ex ante).

[9] Case 27/76, *United Brands Co and United Brands Continental BV v Commission* [1978] ECR I-207, § 65.

[10] Case 85/76, *Hoffmann-La Roche & Co AG v Commission* [1979] ECR I-461, §38.

[11] Case 85/76 *Hoffman-La Roche & Co AG v Commission of the European Communities* [1979] ECR-461 § 41.

The statement from *Hoffman-La Roche* contains no definition of what is implied by the term 'some time'. Thus, the lack of a consistent definition might result in an arbitrary interpretation.

The legal definition of dominance has been addressed by several cases brought before the ECJ. In *Continental Can*,[12] the Commission, in defining a 'dominant position', focused on the ability of entities to behave independently in making decisions that affect the market as a whole. Regarding its definition in merger cases, the formulation of the concept of dominance in *United Brands* was echoed in the ECJ's *Kali-Salz*[13] decision with respect to collective dominance.[14]

The legal definition of dominance as it has emerged through the case law still entails certain drawbacks. The essence of the ECJ's definition of dominance is the ability to act independently to an appreciable extent of competitors, customers and consumers. It is this essence that entails problems. One of the criticisms of the definition of dominance is that firms cannot act to an appreciable extent independently of their consumers, due to the downward-sloping demand curve which implies that the higher the price of the product the lower the quantity demanded. We should note that this inverse relationship between price and quantity may not hold for products such as medicines that are 'price inelastic', meaning that the increase in price may not affect the quantity demanded. This argument holds both for dominant and non-dominant firms, and as Azevedo and Walker (2002) argue, 'trying to define dominance with respect to the ability of a firm to behave to an appreciable extent independently of its consumers will not distinguish adequately between dominant and non-dominant firms'.[15]

[12] Case 6/72 *Europemballage Corp and Continental Can Co Inc v Commission (Continental Can)* [1973] ECR I-215, § 3.

[13] Case M308 *Kali und Salz/MdK/Treuhand* [1998] OJ C275/3; on appeal Cases 68/94 and C-30/95 *France v Commission, Societe Commerciale es Potasses et de l'Azore (SCPA) v Commission* [1998] ECR I-1375.

[14] See § 221 of case C-68/94 and C-30/95 *France v Commission, Societe Commerciale es Potasses et de l'Azore (SCPA) v Commission* [1998] ECR I-1375. According to this paragraph, in the case of an alleged collective dominant position, the Commission is therefore obliged to assess, using a prospective analysis of the reference market, whether the concentration which has been referred to it leads to a situation in which effective competition in the relevant market is significantly impeded by the undertakings involved in the concentration and one or more other undertakings which together, in particular because of correlative factors which exist between them, are able to adopt a common policy on the market and act to a considerable extent independently of their competitors, their customers, and also of consumers.

[15] J P Azevedo, M Walker, 'Dominance: Meaning and Measurement' [2002] 23(7) ECLR 363–367, 364. Additional work on the same definition on dominance includes: F Dethmers, N Dodoo, 'The Abuse of Hoffmann-La Roche: the Meaning of Dominance under EC Competition Law' [2006] 27(10) ECLR 537–549, A Jones and B Sufrin, *EC Competition Law* (2nd edn, Oxford University Press, 2004) 264, J Church and R Ware, *Industrial Organization Strategic Approach* (McGraw-Hill, Singapore, 2000) 603, Cabral L, *Introduction to Industrial Organization* (The MIT Press, Cambridge Massachusetts, 2000) 72–75, I Dobbs, P Richards, 'Output Restriction as a Measure of Market Power' [2005] 26(10) ECLR 572–580.

A further criticism related to the difficulty in measuring the ability of firms to behave independently from competitors. Every firm that faces competitors (ie all firms apart from monopolists) is constrained to some extent by the conduct of these competitors. The pricing policy of even a dominant firm is dependent on the pricing of its competitors. A dominant firm will raise prices above the competitive level to a point that will be determined by its demand curve, as well as by the constraints imposed on the firm by its competitors' strategy. A firm's commercial decisions will take into account its rivals' likely reactions and may adapt its strategy accordingly. So the dominant firm does not act independently of its competitors. This argument is also true in case the market is focused on other dimensions of competition such as quality and innovation.[16]

Azevedo and Walker (2002) argue that the definition of dominance as was outlined in *United Brands* could be made more economically coherent by replacing the 'behave to an appreciable extent independently' with 'restrained by the independent actions'.[17] They also suggest an approach that mitigates the drawbacks related to the definition of dominance in *United Brands*. They argue that dominance can be defined as the ability to restrict output[18] substantially in the marketplace. Dominant firms have power over price and thus, by restricting output in the market, decrease consumer welfare. According to the authors, focusing on output restriction is consistent with most of the standard factors that are usually considered relevant in the appraisal of dominance.[19] In addition, in cases where the observation of price and costs cannot be easily achieved, concentrating on the ability to reduce quantity may provide an alternative means of assessing dominance. Thus, according to the authors, this definition would be consistent with current practice and would have a firm economic foundation.

However, focusing the definition of dominance on the restriction of output may be considered to be too narrow and possibly inadequate to incorporate conduct that has an adverse impact on competition entailing limited or no output restriction. Adverse effects on competition can be induced due to, among other things, lower quality. Notwithstanding the

[16] As regards quality firms might be lowering quality (and hence costs), but not price, up to the point at which further reductions in quality would not be profitable. As regards innovation firms might be slowing the pace of innovation (and hence R&D expenditures) as far as is consistent with maintaining long run profits. See further: Azevedo J P, Walker M, 'Dominance: Meaning and Measurement', CRA Competition Policy Discussion Papers (2001) 1–8, 4 (available from www.crai.co.uk).

[17] J P Azevedo and M Walker, 'Dominance: Meaning and Measurement' (2002) ECLR 23(4) 366.

[18] The authors clarify that the definition refers to the restriction of total output in the market below its current level.

[19] Factors such as market shares, barriers to entry, barriers to expansion, spare capacity, substitute products. Azevedo and Walker (n 17) 6.

criticisms mentioned above, for the purposes of this book dominance is defined according to ECJ's definition in *United Brands*. In the context of Article 82,[20] as the ECJ in *Continental Can* argued, 'there is no need for a causal link to be established between the dominant position and the abuse. It is necessary only that the conduct strengthens the undertaking's dominant position and fetters competition on the market'.[21]

The respondents to the ICN Report cited two basic legal definitions of single-firm dominance/substantial market power—structural and behavioral. Behavioural definitions share a focus on a firm's appreciable freedom from competitive constraints or the ability to act in ways that a competitively constrained firm could not. The structural definition identifies substantial market power by an established market share threshold that may allow for possible situation specific deviations.

Thus, the structural definition identifies dominance by an established market share threshold that may allow for possible situation-specific deviations. Behavioural definitions broadly focus on a firm's appreciable freedom from competitive constraints or ability to act in ways that a competitively-constrained firm could not.

As regards the definition of 'abuse', although there is no definition of the concept in legislation the ECJ has on numerous occasions dealt with this concept; for instance, in *Continental Can*,[22] it stated that 'abuse may occur if an undertaking in a dominant position strengths such position in such a way that the degree of dominance reached substantially fetters competition [that] only undertakings remain in the market whose behaviour depends on the dominant one'.

In *Hoffmann-La Roche*[23] the ECJ widened the concept by holding it to be an 'objective concept' relating to the *behaviour of a dominant undertaking* which *influences the structure of the market* thereby *weakening competition* through methods different from those of normal practice and having an *effect of hindering the maintenance and the growth of competition.* A dominant undertaking can, however, protect its commercial interests, but,

[20] On the contrary as the ECJ confirmed in *Kali und Salz*, there must be a causal link between the creation or the strengthening of dominance under the original ECMR and the adverse impact on effective competition. This distinction on the necessity of the 'causal link' illustrates the different application of the dominance test under Article 82 and ECMR. Case M308 *Kali und Salz/MdK/Treuhand* [1998] OJ C275/3; on appeal Cases 68/94 and C-30/95 *France v Commission, Societe Commerciale es Potasses et de l'Azore (SCPA) v Commission* [1998] ECR I-1375.

[21] Case 6/72 *Europemballage Corp and Continental Can Co Inc v Commission* (Continental Can) [1973] ECR I-215, § 26–§27.

[22] *Europemballage Corp and Continental Can Co Inc v Commission (Continental Can)* § 26.

[23] Case 85/76, *Hoffmann-La Roche & Co AG v Commission* [1979] ECR I-461, § 91, repeated in eg Case 322/81, *Michelin v Commission* [1983] ECR 3461, § 70.

the behaviour must be proportionate and not be intended to strengthen the dominant position and thereby abuse it.[24]

The concept of abuse is related to the behaviour of an undertaking which is such to influence the degree of competition through methods different from those ensuring normal competition. Normal competition refers to a situation where an undertaking has a substantial market share resulting from efficient performance regarding quality of product, of service, efficient marketing and distribution. The first two paragraphs of Article 82 refer to exploitative abuse of market power inducing harm to consumers. The final two refer to methods detrimental to consumers through their impact on effective competition structure.[25]

Existence of a dominant position is a necessary condition for application of Article 82; however, it is not necessary for there to be a link between the dominance and the abuse. As mentioned above, the CFI in the *Continental Can* argued that 'there is no need for a causal link to be established between the dominant position and the abuse. It is necessary only that the conduct strengthens the undertaking's dominant position and fetters competition on the market'[26]. Consequently, a dominant undertaking can abuse its position without using the market power that the position confers, but by ordinary commercial practices also engaged in by non-dominant undertakings.[27] The market in which the abusive conduct takes place need not be the same as that on which the dominant position is held;[28] although the alleged abusive conduct is normally found on the dominated market, it may also be found on a distinct, but closely associated market, likely to strengthen the position on the dominated market.[29]

[24] eg *Europemballage Corp and Continental Can Co Inc v Commission (Continental Can)* § 189.

[25] *Europemballage Corp and Continental Can Co Inc v Commission (Continental Can)* § 26.

[26] *Europemballage Corp and Continental Can Co Inc v Commission (Continental Can)* § 26–§27, fn 4.

[27] *Europemballage Corp and Continental Can Co Inc v Commission (Continental Can)* § 27; Case 85/76, *Hoffmann-La Roche & Co AG v Commission* [1979] ECR I-461, § 91 and § 120.

[28] Case T-51/89, *Tetra Pak Rausing SA v Commission (Tetra Pak I)* [1990] ECR II-309, [1991] 4 CMLR 334, § 25.

[29] Case T-83/91, *Tetra Pak Rausing SA v Commission (Tetra Pak II) [1994]* ECR II-755, § 23–28.

CHAPTER 3

Abuse of Superior Bargaining Position/ Abuse of Economic Dependence

Röller[1] identifies some important 'gaps' in Article 82. Since Article 82 only applies to firms that are *already* dominant, anti-competitive conduct that *leads* to a dominant position cannot be caught in Europe under Article 82 as an exclusionary abuse.[2] This is according to Röller an enforcement 'gap'. Gap cases refer to cases where dominance is a *result* of exclusionary conduct, and not the other way around.[3] He adds that there may be other gaps under Article 82, such as anti-competitive conduct below the level of dominance, or anti-competitive behaviour by an oligopoly as well as achieving dominance through government action (eg natural monopolies). This book will only address the gap that relates to anti-competitive conduct of firms that are not dominant.

In the markets where both larger and smaller firms operate, the issue of abuse of superior bargaining position/abuse of economic dependence[4] arises. In several jurisdictions this issue arises, inter alia, in the retail sector after the emergence of large-scale retailers like hypermarkets.[5] In jurisdictions that address the abuse of superior bargaining position, the concept typically includes, but is not limited to, a firm with a stronger market position entering into contractual relations with other firms under substantially more favourable terms. A firm in the superior bargaining position does not necessarily have to be a dominant firm or a firm with significant market

[1] L Röller, 'Exploitative Abuses', in Ehlermann and Marquis (eds), *European Competition Law Annual 2007: A Reformed Approach to Article 82 EC* (Hart Publishing, 2008).

[2] Exclusionary abuses are practices aimed at foreclosing competitors from the market or marginalizing them, ultimately causing harm to consumers. Exploitative abuses involve a dominant firm which exploits the opportunities provided for by its significant market power in order to harm consumers directly, for example by imposing excessive prices.

[3] Röller would suggest that antitrust enforcement against exploitative abuses can be used to close this important gap. 'Exploitative abuse cases should be based on acquiring a dominant position through anti-competitive exclusionary conduct. Overall, there appear to be three main advantages in defining exploitative abuse as acquiring dominance as a result of an exclusionary abuse. First, it is in line with sound economics. Second, it avoids the standard debate on what is "excessive" (which I believe is impossible to define operationally). And third, it closes the gap described above under Article 82.'

[4] The two terms will be used interchangeably.

[5] See further: Seventh Annual Conference of the International Competition Network, Special Program on Abuse of Superior Bargaining Position.

power. Article 82 does not apply to such conduct unless the undertaking concerned is considered to be dominant.[6] Thus, there is a gap in the application of Article 82 to these kinds of conduct, which can induce consumer harm.

Such practices are in some jurisdictions handled by competition authorities, or by other government agencies under non-competition perspectives.[7] In some jurisdictions, such practices are not regulated, and are addressed through private litigation.[8]

An ICN Report on the abuse of superior bargaining position/abuse of economic dependence identified some jurisdictions (and in particular several larger jurisdictions) where intervention is also possible against an undertaking's allegedly anti-competitive unilateral conduct taken in a market in which it does not hold a pre-existing dominant position.[9] Fifteen of the 35 jurisdictions covered by the ICN questionnaire responses allow for potential enforcement action without the need to find a pre-existing dominant position. Eleven of 35 jurisdictions allow for enforcement based on the allegedly anti-competitive conduct of a non-dominant undertaking.[10]

Some of these jurisdictions aim at creating a 'level playing field' for smaller undertakings and thus prohibit stronger undertakings from exploiting positions of economic dependency or economic disparity. Quite a few EU Member States have clauses in their competition legislation that aim to create such level playing field. Such clauses would make it possible to control, inter alia, discriminatory offers or demands by companies or groups of companies which, without having a dominant position, are obligatory partners either for their suppliers or their customers because of their influence in the market.[11] The notion of abuse of economic dependence applies to situations where after defining the market no incumbent can be characterized as being in a dominant position.[12]

[6] And even if the undertaking concerned is dominant, Article 82 may not apply to all its conduct.

[7] US and UK consider this conduct as contractual disputes and not competition-related.

[8] The extent of private litigation depends inter alia on the resources of the involved parties. Private litigations cannot substitute for competition enforcement conducted by the relevant authorities and courts.

[9] Seventh Annual Conference of the International Competition Network, Special Program on Abuse of Superior Bargaining Position.

[10] ICN Kyoto-ASBP, page 61. Annex 3 presents a table of the stages at which competition authorities can intervene in the jurisdictions that responded to the ICN survey. It is interesting to note the number of jurisdictions where competition law enables the competition agency to intervene against unilateral conduct at a level below dominance threshold.

[11] The extent of the possible gap is indicated by the fact that in five years, under the legislation on abuse of economic dependence, the Bundeskartellamt initiated more than one hundred proceedings, for abuse of purchasing power by major distributors. See further: I Roudard, 'The New French legislation on Competition' [1989] 10(2) ECLR 205–232.

[12] Particularly in cases of abuse arising from mass marketing. See further: I Roudard, 'The

The legislation and case law related to the abuse of superior bargaining position/abuse of economic dependence will be analysed in this section. The Member States which have clauses dealing with such abuse can enforce their national legislation to prevent, inter alia, non-dominant firms from adopting anti-competitive conduct. Thus, they can capture conduct that the EC cannot under the current application of Article 82. Such infringements will not require that an undertaking holds a dominant position in a given market in order for it to be guilty of an abuse; it will suffice that there are third parties in a situation of economic dependency, which do not have an alternative. The exploitation of a situation of economic dependence may be presumed, for example, whenever a supplier is compelled on a regular basis to grant the purchaser not only ordinary discounts, but also other advantages not available to other purchasers. Abuse of economic dependence does not require that a dominant position in the national market or in a substantial part of it exists, but only a situation of economic dependence or relative dominance towards other commercial partners.

Under EC law, abuses of superior bargaining power are, in principle, governed by Article 82. There are no separate laws that relate or refer to the concept of 'superior bargaining position'. It can therefore be presumed that all anti-competitive conduct, whether or not in the context of business-to-business bargaining, falls under Article 82. However, only abusive behaviour performed by a dominant firm can constitute an infringement. Dominance assessment thus serves as a filter when analysing unilateral conduct cases. And this is where the gap in the application of Article 82 lies.

The Commission and the CFI/ECJ do not appear to have extensively addressed the issue of the abuse of economic dependence in the case law. The concept of economic dependence has been used in some cases in order to indicate the dependence of customers on the firms under investigation. It has been employed as a factor indicating dominance,[13] but has never, to this author's knowledge, been the basis for the sustainability of an allegation of anti-competitive behaviour by non-dominant firms.

According to Schodermeier (1990), in the cases *ABG*[14] and *Magill*[15] the Commission did not base its analysis on the fact alone that the oligopolists had acted in a parallel manner. It also relied on the findings, inter alia, that potential customers found themselves in a position of economic dependence vis-à-vis the oligopolists. In *Magill,* the Commission looked at the economic

New French legislation on competition' [1989] 10(2) ECLR 205–232. As mentioned above, if the third biggest firm's market share is similar to the top two, the same arguments as regards the consumer harm induced by adopting possible anti-competitive conduct can be made.

13 See further: J Shaw, 'Inter versus intra brand competition: dominant positions and ancillary markets' [1987] 12(3) E L Rev 12(3) 195–199.

14 (1977) OJ L 117/1.

15 (1989) OJ L 78/43. See § 22.

dependence of third parties on the broadcasting organizations. It stated that the broadcasting organizations had a factual monopoly over the production and publication of their weekly listings. Thus, a monopolistic situation existed in which the broadcasting organizations had the sole access and control over the essential input—the advance weekly listings—for which there was no readily available substitute.[16] Vogel (1998) has also argued that the ECJ in *Hugin v Commission*,[17] in which a supplier who refused to provide independent repairers with spare parts for the products it made, claiming that it had set up its own repair service, was considered to have abused its dominant position on the market for spare parts for its own products. The court ruling actually condemned an abuse of economic dependence, rather than abuse of a dominant position.[18]

The EC has acknowledged and respected, in Regulation 1/2003, the ability of the Member States to apply stricter rules than Article 82. Article 3 of Regulation 1/2003 does not compromise the application of specific national law provisions permitting Member States to address specific issues with which EC law can not deal appropriately. These national laws in some EU jurisdictions tackle the abuse of economic dependence.[19]

According to Gilliams (2003), one example of such anti-competitive conduct and of allowing national laws to be stricter than Article 82 is the French prohibition against 'abusive exploitation of economic dependence', which applies even in the absence of a dominant position. The eighth recital of the preamble of Regulation 1/2003 contains a veiled reference to this provision.[20] The Conseil de la Concurrence,[21] provided a non-exhaustive list of the criteria which can be used to determine the existence of dependence: how well-known the supplier's brand is, for certain products; the size of the supplier's market share for these products; the proportion represented by these products in the reseller's turnover or else the proportion of the supplier's deliveries in the reseller's supplies; finally, the possibility or impossibility of the distributor obtaining equivalent products in identical conditions from other suppliers or wholesalers. The presumption of dependence merely requires the combination of a sufficient number of these criteria.[22]

[16] D Price, 'Abuse of a Dominant Position—the Tale of Nails, Milk Cartons and TV Guides' [1990] 11(2) ECLR 80–90.

[17] C-22/78, *Hugin v European Commission* [1979] ECR I-1869.

[18] L Vogel (1998), 'Competition Law and Buying Power: the Case for a New Approach in Europe' [1998] 19(1) ECLR 4–11.

[19] Article 3(2) does not specify expressly Article 82 as the comparator for the 'stricter' national law and it does not refer to dominance. Recital 8 gives as an illustration of stricter national laws prohibiting unilateral conduct.

[20] H Gilliams, 'Modernisation: from Policy to Practice' [2003] 28(4) E L Rev 451–474.

[21] First report of the activities of the Conseil de la Concurrence for 1987, at XXII.

[22] See further: First report of the activities of the Conseil de la Concurrence for 1987, at XXII and I Roudard, 'The New French Legislation on Competition' [1989] 10(2) ECLR 205–232.

The range of anti-competitive conduct that can constitute an abuse of economic dependence is varied and includes non-cost justified rebates, entry fees, listing fees, shelf rental payments and other charges, which are enforced by the buyer after the original contract has been signed and agreed (ie mainly forms of post-contractual opportunistic behaviour). The adoption of restrictive practices or termination of established business relationships without cause, taking into account the nature of such relationships and the recognized business practices applicable to any such business, may be considered as an abuse of economic dependence.

The Member States that apply such laws differ in market and economic characteristics. Thus, the application of such legislation does not stem from features particular to the country and/or economy but stem from the willingness of these countries to be able to address anti-competitive conduct by non-dominant firms. In what follows we will review some of these laws as well as cases under these laws in order to clearly prove the gap in the application of Article 82 due to its inapplicability to abuses of superior bargaining position/abuse of economic dependence.[23]

We will assess how the concept of abuse of superior bargaining position/abuse of economic dependence is applied in several EU jurisdictions. The sample includes large and smaller economies, as well as older and newer Member States.[24]

[23] In Luxembourg, the 2004 Law does not provide for any rules applying to conduct of non-dominant firms. However, the Law of 30 July 2002, governing certain commercial practices and prohibiting unfair competition, prohibits unfair practices, such as sale at loss, independently of the fact that the relevant undertaking is in a dominant position or not. Law on Competition of 17 May 2004 (the '2004 Law'). http://www.legilux.public.lu/leg/a/archives/2004/0762605/0762605.pdf?SID=9c660fa1e8e5446d8be91743b21d36cb#page=2.

In Spain Article 6(1) of the Competition Act (Law 16/1989, of July 17) described the prohibition of abusive behaviour in the market by dominant companies as 'the abusive exploitation by one or more companies of: (a) its/their dominant position in all or part of the national market; (b) the situation of economic dependence in which its/their client or supplier undertakings may be, in so far as they do not have an equivalent alternative to conduct their business. This situation will be presumed when apart from regular discounts, a supplier has to grant other additional advantages on a regular basis that are not granted to similar purchasers'. E Navarro Varona (2000), 'Amendments to the Spanish Law for the Defence of Competition' [2000] 21(4) ECLR 235–238. The main proposals put forward by the White Paper were aimed at the harmonisation of Spanish legislation with EC competition rules. In particular, the White Paper suggested: (i) the disappearance or clarification of two separate anti-competitive conduct under Spanish law consisting of the abuse of a situation of economic dependence and unfair conduct affecting competition. In the new Competition Act 15/2007, of 3 July 2007 (http://www.cncompetencia.es/PDFs/doc/P_63.pdf), article 2 which relate to abuse of dominant position does not refer to conduct of non-dominant firms. See further: H Armengod, 'A White Book for the Reform of the Spanish Competition Law System' [2005] ECLR, P Callol, P Pignatelli (2005), 'Spain: General—Competition Enforcement' [2005] 26(5) ECLR N71–72.

[24] In Italy abuse of superior bargaining position can be addressed through a private civil action for injunctive relief and compensation for breach of section 9 of Law no 192 of 18 June 1998. This law which applies only to business-to-business relations prevents firms from

Before we analyse the precedents in the Member States, we should note the practice of the Commission and the CFI/ECJ in addressing anti-competitive conduct in cases where there are undertakings that customers are dependent on for the supply of goods or services. In *Deutsche Bahn v Commission*[25] the CFI upheld the Commission's decision, and emphasized the economic dependence of railway operators on the statutory monopolist for the provision of railway services within Germany.

The CFI stated:

> '[I]t is clear from the case-law that where, as in the present case, the services covered by the sub-market are the subject of a statutory monopoly, placing those seeking the services in a position of economic dependence on the supplier, the existence of a dominant position on a distinct market cannot be denied, even if the services provided under a monopoly are linked to a product which is itself in competition with other products'.[26]

In addition in the *BA/Virgin*[27] case the Commission argued that British Airways was an unavoidable trading partner for travel agents in the markets for air transport. We can thus argue that the economic dependence to an undertaking which can behave independently can provide this undertaking the ability to prevent competition.

A. Germany

The German legislator, when incorporating para 20(2) ARC into antitrust law in 1973, held the view that not only conduct by those undertakings holding a dominant position could distort competition. In fact, conduct by undertakings which were able to exercise market power only to a certain extent and in relation to certain undertakings, was also deemed to be capable of having negative effects on competition.[28]

Paragraph 20 extends the prohibition of discriminatory practices and the prohibition of unfair hindrance to non-dominant undertakings with relative market power in relation to small and medium-sized suppliers or purchasers, and to non-dominant undertakings with superior market power in relation to small and medium-sized competitors.[29]

exploiting economic dependence of their customers or suppliers. The Italian Competition Authority can intervene only if the alleged abuse of economic dependence also has an impact on the protection of competition and the market.

25 Case T-229/94 *Deutsche Bahn v Commission* [1997] ECR II-1689.

26 Case T-229/94 *Deutsche Bahn v Commission* [1997] ECR II-1689 para 57.

27 *BA/Virgin* [2000] OJ L 30/1.

28 http://www.icn-kyoto.org/documents/germany.pdf. ICN Kyoto-ASBP, 3.

29 Examples of conduct that constitutes abuse of superior bargaining position in Germany include demanding retrospective rebates, refusal to supply undertakings with 'must-stock'

According to paragraph 20:

> (1) Dominant undertakings, associations of competing undertakings within the meaning of §§ 2, 3 and 28 (1) and undertakings set retail prices pursuant to § 28 (2), or § 30 (1) sentence 1, shall not directly or indirectly hinder in an unfair manner another undertaking in business activities which are usually open to similar undertakings, nor directly or indirectly treat it differently from similar undertakings without any objective justification.
> (2) Paragraph 1 shall also apply to undertakings and associations of undertakings insofar as small or medium-sized enterprises as suppliers or purchasers of certain kinds of goods or commercial services depend on them in such a way that sufficient and reasonable possibilities of resorting to other undertakings do not exist. A supplier of a certain kind of goods or commercial services shall be presumed to depend on a purchaser within the meaning of sentence 1 if this purchaser regularly obtains from this supplier, in addition to discounts customary in the trade or other remuneration, special benefits which are not granted to similar purchasers.

The provision subjects so-called 'market strong' undertakings to the same obligations placed upon market-dominant undertakings by section 20 paragraph 1 GWB. Section 20 paragraph 1 GWB deviates most from its European equivalents. Section 20 paragraph 1 GWB is the most prominent German example of the application of the permission granted by Article 3 paragraph 2 of Council Regulation (EC) No 1/2003, according to which Member States may adopt and apply on their territory stricter national laws which prohibit or sanction unilateral conduct engaged in by undertakings.[30]

Section 20 paragraph 2 subjects to competition legislation enterprises that are only relatively powerful and which do not dominate the market concerned.[31] Paragraph 20(2), sentence 2 ARC provides for a presumption

items, abusive and unjustified setting of sales prices by a franchisor, agreements on an exclusive purchasing obligation within a franchising system purchasing benefits are not passed on to the franchisee, manufacturers requiring trading firms to comply with their provisions in terms of quantities and turnovers on the type of resale; eg the setting of a maximum threshold for internet sales without any objective justification, deliberate non-disclosure of interface information in the software sector by a car manufacturer. See further: ICN Kyoto-ASBP Germany response.

30 Chapter on Germany by Reiner Bechtold and Ulrich Denzel in I Kokkoris, *Competition Cases from the European Union* (Sweet and Maxwell, London, 2007).

31 Immenga and Mestmäcker—Markert, Kommentar zum GWB (1st edn, 1981) § 26, No 115 et seq; Schödermeier M, *Metro II et les Limites de la Distribution Sélective* (Cahiers de Droit Européen (hereinafter CDE) 1987) 681 ff, 692. See further: M Schodermeier (1990), 'Collective Dominance Revisited: an Analysis of the EC Commission's New Concepts of Oligopoly Control' [1990] 11(1) ECLR 28–34.

of a superior bargaining position. According to the law, a supplier of a certain kind of goods or commercial services shall be presumed to depend on a purchaser within the meaning of § 20 (2) sentence 1 ARC if this purchaser regularly obtains from this supplier, in addition to discounts customary in the trade or other remuneration, special benefits which are not granted to similar purchasers.[32] This provision extends the obligations placed upon market-dominant undertakings by section 20 paragraph 1 GWB to those undertakings which—although they are not dominant—enjoy a special market position in so far as small or medium-sized enterprises depend on them since they do not have sufficient and reasonable possibilities of resorting to other undertakings.

The relationship of the provisions relevant to abuse of dominance position and to abuse of superior bargaining position is very close. The latter provision (section 20 paragraph 2) refers to the provision governing the conduct of dominant firms (section 20 paragraph 1). As Germany's response to the ICN Report-ASBP mentions, section 20 paragraph 2 widens the scope of application of section 20 paragraph 1 with the effect that not only dominant but also such firms with a superior bargaining position are prohibited from unfairly hindering business partners which depend on them.

The German Competition Act also adds that an unfair hindrance of small and medium-sized competitors includes cases where an undertaking offers goods or commercial services not merely occasionally below its cost price, unless there is an objective justification.[33]

Dependence of *small or medium-sized enterprises* on *undertakings and associations of undertakings* exists only if besides the undertaking allegedly holding a superior bargaining position in the relevant market, no other undertakings exist which would be able and willing to supply the respective small or medium-sized undertaking on reasonable terms. Such dependence may be evident where: (i) a wholesaler/retailer needs to stock certain branded goods in order to be competitive and profitable; (ii) switching would be possible[34] but should be subject to severe competitive disadvantages if a supplier or customer has adapted his sales or purchases to one single contractual partner or if there is a general shortage of goods.

Conduct which constitutes an abuse of superior bargaining position includes:[35]

32 ICN response to Kyoto.
33 § 20(4).
34 Switching may not be occurring at all.
35 See ICN Kyoto-ASBP, 21.

a) demanding retrospective rebates (so called 'tapping a company for rebates');
b) refusal to supply undertakings with 'must-stock' items;
c) abusive and unjustified setting of sales prices by a franchisor;
d) agreements on an exclusive purchasing obligation within a franchising system;
e) purchasing benefits are not passed on to the franchisee;
f) manufacturers requiring trading firms to comply with their provisions in terms of quantities and turnovers on the type of resale; eg the setting of a maximum threshold for internet sales without any objective justification;
g) deliberate non-disclosure of interface information in the software sector by a car manufacturer; and
h) the use of pressure.

According to Schodermeier (1990),[36] the meaning of this section can be highlighted by the practice of the German courts: in several cases they have established the existence of dependence in the sense of section 26(2)(2), although several undertakings competed vigorously in the market concerned.[37] Section 26(2)(2) of the GWB therefore concentrated the analysis on the specific relationships between powerful undertakings and their customers and was less concerned about the structure of the market in general. Thus, the analysis was focused less on the structural features of the market (eg market shares) but rather on the ensuing harm to consumers as a result of the adoption of anti-competitive conduct.[38]

Rossignol[39] is one of the most eminent cases regarding the concept of abuse of superior bargaining power. Rossignol which was a case of 'single

[36] Schodermeier focuses his analysis on a previous version of the German Act (section 26(2)(2)), which in substance addressed the same concept. The German cases referred herein as examples of application under the previous version of the GWB are useful in substantiating the importance of the existence of such legislation in order to capture anti-competitive conduct of non-dominant firms.

[37] BGH WuW/E 2125, 2127 Nordmende Stuttgart Court of Appeal WuW/E OLG 4047, 4049 Blaupunkt, Berlin Court of Appeal, AG 1987, 285, 291 COOP/Wandmaker.

[38] Between 1997 and 2007 the Bundeskartellamt examined 39 cases of 'abuse of superior bargaining position'. Three of these cases ended with a decision that the conduct violated antitrust rules:
—Praktiker Baumärkte/Franchisesystem (2006)
—RMS Radio/Aachener Lokalsender (2001)
—Metro MGE Einkaufs GmbH (1999)
Another five cases ended in a settlement with relief (without a formal decision):
—Sternjakob/Schulranzen (2006)
—Adam Opel AG/Software DMS (2006)
—Karstadt Quelle AG (2003).
See the German Response to ICN Kyoto-ASBP for analysis of some of these cases.

[39] KZR 1/75 (Rossignol, November 20, 1975) WuW/E BGH 1391. See further: Chapter on Germany in I Kokkoris (n 30).

firm dependency' ('*Spitzenstellungsabhängigkeit*'), describing a situation in which, in order to be competitive, the small or medium-sized undertaking in question (in the case at hand a sports shop in Upper Bavaria) had to be supplied with the products of one particular supplier (in the case at hand, Rossignol skis) because these products were so important that they could not be replaced by the products of other suppliers.

The sports shop and the German subsidiary of Rossignol had a long-standing business relationship. Rossignol announced that it would no longer supply the sports shop. The subsequent lawsuit between the sports shop and Rossignol concerned the legal question of whether Rossignol was obliged to supply the sports shop and whether it was liable for any damages incurred by the sports shop due to Rossignol's refusal to supply. After conflicting decisions of the lower courts, the Bundesgerichtshof decided that Rossignol, as a 'market strong' undertaking within the meaning of section 20 paragraph 2 GWB (at the time: section 26 paragraph 2 GWB), was obliged to supply the sports shop and had to compensate it for damages.

In the light of Rossignol's market share of about 8 per cent, the Bundesgerichtshof denied—for lack of a market-dominating position—that Rossignol had a supply obligation according to section 20 paragraph 1 GWB.

However, the Court upheld Rossignol's obligation to supply the sports shop under section 20, paragraph 2 GWB. The Court identified the element of dependence as the crucial part of the wording of section 20 paragraph 2 GWB and stated that the obligations provided for by the provision had to be determined by construing whether the small or medium-sized enterprise wishing to be supplied had 'sufficient and reasonable possibilities of resorting to other undertakings'. Whether this was the case had to be determined primarily by objective criteria and in particular by assessing the relevance of alternative possible sources of supply.

In general terms, section 20 paragraph 2 GWB provides that undertakings are 'market strong' if and in so far as small or medium-sized enterprises depend on them for not having sufficient and reasonable possibilities of resorting to other undertakings. The German practice distinguishes between different sorts of dependency, the most important being the so-called '*sortimentsbedingte Abhängigkeit*' which is present if a small or medium-sized undertaking is dependent on being supplied with the products of one or several suppliers in order to be competitive on the downstream market.

The *Designer-Polstermöbel* case[40] represents another application of section 20 paragraph 2 GWB. This case involved a small or medium-sized undertaking (a dealer in upholstery furniture) which was dependent on the

40 KZR 28/98, Designer-Polstermöbel (9 May 2000) WuW/E DE-R 481.

products of a group of top manufacturers in its portfolio and was thus dependent on the group of manufacturers. As such, Designer-Polstermöbel is the leading case for an application concerning the 'group dependency' doctrine ('*Spitzengruppenabhängigkeit*').[41]

In most cases, section 20 paragraph 2 GWB gives rise to the obligation of a manufacturer to supply certain undertakings of the demand side. However, the provision can also work to the advantage of suppliers. The *Importarzneimittel* case[42] is an example of such a situation. At the centre of the Bundesgerichtshof's decision in the *Importarzneimittel* case is the finding that, where all undertakings at a certain trading level refuse to procure from the small or medium-sized undertaking, the latter may be considered to be dependent on each and every one of them and that 'dependency' within the meaning of the provision does not presuppose that the undertaking in question is not economically viable at all if not accepted as a purchaser or supplier by the market-strong undertaking(s), but that substantial competitive disadvantages vis-à-vis its competitors can suffice for a finding of dependency.[43]

B. France

Under French law, the abuse of a dominant position is not the only form of illegal abuse.[44] Article L. 420-2, paragraph 2 CC prohibits:

> The abuse by an undertaking or group of undertakings of the state of economic dependence in which a client or supplier undertaking finds itself in respect of the above shall also be prohibited *when it is likely to affect the operation or structure of competition*. These abuses may in particular consist of refusals to sell, linked sales or the discriminatory practices referred to in Article L.442-6.[45,46]

[41] Chapter on Germany in I Kokkoris (n 30).

[42] KVR 10/94, Importarzneimittel (21 February 1995) WuW/E BGH 2990.

[43] The analysis of this case is taken from the chapter on Germany in I Kokkoris (n 106).

[44] The most recent decision that relates to the abuse of an economic dependence in France is Decision No.04-D-44 dated 15 September 2004. Abuse of economic dependence should not be confused with abuses in the relation to dependence, which is considered as a restrictive trade practice (contractual or tort perspective).

[45] Act No 2001-420 of 15 May 2001, Article 66, Official Gazette of 16 May 2001.

[46] Indeed, Article L 442-6 consists in a list of per se prohibited restrictive trade practices, which, until very recently, used to include unjustified discrimination. This particular prohibition has been lifted by the recent of 'modernization of the economy' voted in August 2008. Other prohibited practices include: disproportionate commercial obligations (formerly abuse of trade dependence), subjecting a partner to unjustified obligations or trading conditions, sudden severance (or threat of) of established business relations, subjecting a partner to manifestly unfair terms of payment, automatic debiting of suppliers by distributors, among others. Unlike the abuse of economic dependence featured in Article L. 420-2, these prohibitions are

Competition law in France sanctions abuses of economic dependence, no prior determination of dominance being necessary. Abuses of economic dependence can include: refusal to sell, bundled sales, discrimination, certain types of bundled purchase agreements, and, most often, abrupt cessation or alteration of commercial relationships.

The French Competition Council has considered that:

> [S]ituations of dependence arise within bilateral relationships between two firms and must therefore be assessed on a case by case basis, and not a general basis for a profession as a whole.[47]

Four cumulative criteria are used to assess dependence. In the case of a distributor alleging to be dependent of his supplier, these criteria will be: the reputation of the supplier's product; the supplier's market share; the supplier's market share in his distributor's turnover; and the absence of any alternative solution for the distributor.

As an illustration, the Competition Council reviewed the complaint[48] filed by the company Daniel Grenin, specializing in road-hauling and the storage of goods, against two of its customers (IUP/SM).[49]

Two of its customers had decided to cease using Daniel Grenin's goods storage services, informed it of this decision in December 1999, and cut all business ties with it in January 2000. At the same time, the companies in question had stopped using Daniel Grenin's road-hauling services but without informing it, even though it had already given them a significant rate cut.

The Competition Council indicated that the state of economic dependence stems from an aggregation of cumulative criteria:

- notoriety of the supplier's brand;
- importance of the supplier's market share;
- significance of the supplier's market share in the sales figures of the company in question, provided this market share is not the result of a deliberate choice by the corporate customer;

enforced on a per se basis, regardless of their impact on competition: their objective is to protect the fairness of commercial relationships. As such, the restrictive trade practices fall within the jurisdiction of regular courts and are not enforced by the French Competition Council, unless they also constitute an abuse of economic dependence as defined in Article L 420-2.

[47] Decision 03-D-42 of August 18, 2003 (translation). For additional cases dealing with abuse of economic dependence see further: L Luce Nollet, Y Utzschneider, 'France: Award of Radio Frequency Licences not subject to Jurisdiction of Competition Authority' [2002] ECLR N26-27, *France Telecom SA v Numericable SNC* [2001] ECC 2.

[48] L Nollet, 'France: Anti-Competitive Practices' [2003] 24(7) ECLR N116-117.

[49] All subsidiaries of the Usinor Groupage.

- difficulty for the company to find other suppliers of equivalent products.[50]

Applying the four criteria defined above—Daniel Grenin's firm is considered here as a distributor—the Competition Council considered that Daniel Grenin was able to offset the noted reduction by means of other activities; indeed, even though the share of its turnover attributable to IUP had been decreasing for three years, Daniel Grenin's total turnover had remained fairly constant. The complaint for abuse of economic dependence was therefore dismissed.

In a case involving a franchise agreement for a supermarket operated under a trade name belonging to the Promodès Group, the Cour de Cassation concluded, first of all, that the franchisee was in a position of economic dependence as its purchases of supplies from the franchiser represented two thirds of the value of its turnover. The court then held that the franchisor abused this dependence by taking responsibility for the management and accounting services of the franchised store, in return for a substantial increase in the franchise fees. In addition, the franchisee was obliged to place orders without prior knowledge of purchase prices.[51] Thus, the franchisor acted in a manner contrary to the franchisee's interests. The court also held that, due to the unlimited term of the agreement, the franchisee was unable to safeguard itself from the influence of the franchisor, as termination of the agreement would inevitably lead to the termination of the management leasing agreement, thus resulting in the franchisee being effectively prevented from using any alternative sources of supply.[52]

In another case, the Cour de Cassation on an appeal brought by a distributor of audiovisual products against the dismissal of its claims that the respondent supplier had abused the state of economic dependence stated that for a distributor, a state of economic dependence was defined as the situation in which an undertaking had no opportunity of replacing its supplier or suppliers so as to meet its demand for stock on comparable technical and economic terms. The mere fact that a distributor obtained a very large proportion, or even all, of its stock from a single supplier was not enough to establish a state of economic dependence within the meaning of Art.L.420-2 of the Code.[53]

[50] L Nollet, 'France: Anti-competitive Practices' [2003] 24(7) ECLR N116-117. The last criterion is normally the decisive one.

[51] The franchisor also attempted and in fact obtained a power of attorney and a banking signature from its franchisee.

[52] Y Utzschneider, 'France: Franchise Agreement—Position of Economic Dependence' [1998] 19(5) ECLR N82.

[53] *Concurrence SA v Sony SA* [2005] ECC 4.

The French authorities will apply the four abovementioned criteria in judging whether a particular conduct constitutes an abuse of economic dependence. Each complaint received which meets these four criteria will be assumed that it entails economic dependence. After substantiating the existence of economic dependence the authorities will examine whether there is an abuse and whether the abuse affects competition. Complaints which meet the 'economic dependence' and the 'abuse' criteria are likely to also have an adverse impact on competition and thus will be investigated further by the authorities. Since 1986, there have been between 40 and 50 complaints investigated which led to seven condemnation decisions.

C. Portugal

The Portuguese legislation prohibits the abuse of economic dependence. According to Article 7:

> Abuse of economic dependence
> 1—Insofar as it may affect the functioning of the market or the structure of the competition, one or more undertakings shall not engage in the abusive exploitation of the economic dependence on it or them of any supplier or client on account of the absence of an equivalent alternative.
> 2—The following in particular may be considered abusive:
> a) Any of the forms of behaviour laid out in Article 4 (1)
> b) The unjustified cessation, total or partial, of an established commercial relationship, with due consideration being given to prior commercial relations, the recognised usage in that area of economic activity and the contractual conditions established.
> 3—For the purposes of paragraph 1, an undertaking is understood as having no equivalent alternative when:
> a) The supply of the good or service in question, in particular that of distribution, is provided by a restricted number of undertakings; and
> b) The undertaking cannot obtain identical conditions from other commercial partners in a reasonable space of time.

The Portuguese authority considers that a company is in a situation of economic dependence as regards the supplier or client with whom it contracts an important part of its sales or purchases, when, if the latter wanted to terminate those sales or purchases, it would not be able to find in the market any equivalent product or service. The following criteria support a finding of economic dependence of distributors *vis-à-vis* their suppliers: (i) the notoriety of the trade mark; (ii) the supplier's market share;

(iii) the importance of the supplier's products in the sales of the distributor; and (iv) the absence of an equivalent product.[54]

The abuse of a situation of economic dependence was analysed, for the first time, in two decisions of the Competition Council rendered on 13 July 2000. The cases concerned Unicer (Procedure 2/99), and Centralcer (Procedure 3/98), the two largest beer producers in Portugal.

Both Unicer and Centralcer had entered into exclusive distribution agreements with their distributors, containing exclusivity and non-competition obligations, as well as other non-contractual obligations (dress code of the distributor's professionals, the type, design and colour of their cars and the inclusion of the producer's trademark publicity in such cars). Unicer and Centralcer were accused of having abused the economic dependence of their distributors, by: (i) Unicer having unilaterally without notice amended or terminated agreements with some of its distributors, after having required them to make investments which could not be recovered before the date of the amendments/termination; and (ii) Centralcer having initiated, in the same area where its exclusive distributors were operating, direct sales to important retailers who had significant market power.[55]

The Competition Council was of the opinion that, despite the fact that it is not expressly outlined in the legislation, one may only consider that an abuse of economic dependence exists when it has as its object or effect the prevention, restriction or distortion of competition.

D. Greece

In Greece the legislation prohibits the abuse of a relationship of economic dependence. This provision was inserted in this law by article 16 of L. 2000/1991, which added a new paragraph 2a to article 2 of L. 703/1977. It was incorporated as a separate article and substituted by article 1(2) of L. 2296/1995. It was abolished by article 1(1) of L. 2837/2000, and came into force again by the aforementioned article 1 of L. 3373/2005.

According to this provision, the abuse of a relationship of economic dependence by one or more undertakings connected with an undertaking acting as a client or supplier of a particular kind of product or service, which has no equivalent alternative, is prohibited. This abuse of a relationship of economic dependence may particularly consist in imposing arbitrary

[54] As to the fourth criterion, it must be analysed objectively (ie if there are, in the market, other supply alternatives) and subjectively (ie whether such alternatives are economically practicable for the relevant distributor).

[55] C P Correia, P Pinheiro, 'Portugal: Exploitation of Economic Dependence' [2001] 22(8) ECLR N117-119.

trading terms, applying a discriminatory treatment, or suddenly and unjustifiably terminating longtime commercial relations.[56]

The following criteria are required in order to satisfy the test of sudden and unjustified termination of long-term economic relations:

a) There must be a relation where an undertaking economically depends on another or other undertakings which are its suppliers of certain products or services.
b) This undertaking does not have an equivalent alternative in the sense that there are no alternatives at all or the ones that are offered have serious disadvantages. There is no other source to supply these products or services, or if there is another source the supply is not made under the same but under less favourable conditions, which place the dependent undertaking in a position less favourable than that of its competitors, since it diminishes considerably its ability to function in a system of free competition, something which may cause the discontinuation of operations even of the undertaking where the others depend
c) There must be an abuse of a relation of economic dependence, namely the relatively dominant undertaking takes advantage of the power given by the weakness of the dependent undertaking which has no other alternative and as a result competitiveness of the latter is seriously hurt.

In the *ES against Karelia Tobacco Industry SA* case,[57] a complaint was filed by ES, a wholesale dealer of cigarettes against Karelia Tobacco Industry SA for infringement of article 2a of L. 703/1977 on the grounds of unjustified termination of their long-term commercial relationship. In the scope of a commercial agency agreement, which was in force for decades, the complainant was entitled to sell to retailer dealers in the agreed territory cigarettes and other tobacco products, produced or distributed by Karelia SA. The latter suddenly terminated the agreement with the complainant by means of a letter, sent on 30 October 1997, where it was stated that termination had effect as of 6 November 1997, due to the reconstruction of the distribution system. It suspended sales of cigarettes and other tobacco products to the agent.

The Competition Commission held that the object of the prohibition of article 2a of L. 703/1977 is not to prolong contractual relations but to provide a reasonable period, within which the depended undertaking will

[56] For cases on abuse of economic dependence see: Decision 38/II/1999, 99/II/1999, 154/II/2000, 156/II/2000. www.epant.gr.

[57] Hellenic Competition Commission No 145/11/2000, ES against Karelia Tobacco Industry SA. The case is from the chapter on Greece authored by Professor Triantafillakis in Kokkoris I (n 30).

have a considerable return on the investments, made in view of this particular commercial relationship and adjust to the new developments. Although it is generally acknowledged that the supplier is entitled to choose or amend the system of distribution of his products, in order to improve his competitive position in the case in question Karelia SA, exercising its right abusively, gave to the complainant who was a business partner for decades, a very short notice (just one week) after termination of the agreement, although it could have given him a deadline of at least six (6) months without prejudice to any of its rights.

The Competition Commission held that the conduct of Karelia SA infringes article 2a of L. 703/ 1977 and ordered Karelia SA to terminate the infringement and supply the tobacco products that it imports, produces and distributes to the complainant on the same conditions that apply to its agents. It also imposed a fine on Karelia SA. The Administrative Appeal Court of Athens, in its judgment No 6009/2001, ruled that the conduct of Karelia SA constitutes an abuse of a relation of economic dependence of ES by Karelia SA in breach of article 2a of L. 703/1977 and upheld the decision of the Competition Commission.

E. Latvia

In Latvia, according to the forthcoming amendments in competition legislation, the definition of dominant position will exclude the market share threshold necessary for identifying dominant position, which is presently set at 40 per cent in the relevant market.[58] A new concept 'significant influence' has also been introduced, which should be distinguished from the concept of dominant position. A company with significant impact might not be able to significantly distort competition or act independently from its competitors, though it is capable to force unfair and discriminatory contract rules or payments upon their suppliers, etc. The significant influence concept will apply only to the buyer side in the relevant retail market in Latvia.

Significant influence refers to the status of those market participants, whose market share exceeds 25 per cent in the relevant retail market but who are not in a dominant position. It refers to an economic position of a market participant or several market participants in the relevant retail market when, exercising an economic activity individually or within the framework of mutually concluded franchise agreements or horizontal agreements, the market share in Latvia of this market participant or these market participants is at least 25 per cent, which is, however, not in a dominant position.[59]

[58] At the time of writing the amendments had not been adopted.

[59] Retail refers selling goods for the individual consumption or utilization, and is not related to provision of services.

The amendments state that it shall be prohibited for a market participant having a significant influence in the relevant retail market to abuse it, by imposing or applying unfair or discriminatory trade provisions to other market participants.

Abuse of significant impact may also occur as:[60]

1) unfair or ungrounded share of responsibility about potential risks between contract parties;
2) unfair or ungrounded application or imposition of payment terms for goods being present in the store unless these payment terms are justified due to promotion of new and unknown to the consumers goods in the market;
3) unfair or ungrounded application or imposition of payment terms for the conclusion of contract unless these payment terms are justified thereof contract is being concluded with a new supplier which wherewith has to be specially evaluated;
4) unfair or ungrounded application or imposition of payment terms for supply of goods to the new store;
5) application or imposition of unfairly or unduly long terms of payment for supplied goods.

F. Ireland

The provisions of section 15B of the Competition Act 2002, as inserted by section 1 of the Competition (Amendment) Act 2006, prohibit certain unilateral conduct by non-dominant undertakings, in the grocery sector, which has as its object or effect the prevention, restriction or distortion of competition in trade in any grocery goods.[61]

[60] ICN Kyoto-ASBP.

[61] A 'grocery goods undertaking' means any undertaking (other than in the restaurant and catering sector) engaged for gain in the production, supply or distribution of food or drink for human consumption.

15B.—(1) Subject to subsection (5), a grocery goods undertaking shall not directly or indirectly attempt to compel or coerce another grocery goods undertaking, whether by threat, promise or any like means, to resell or advertise for resale any grocery goods at—

(a) a price fixed directly or indirectly by the first mentioned grocery goods undertaking, or

(b) a price above a minimum price fixed directly or indirectly by the first mentioned grocery goods undertaking.

(2) Subject to subsection (5), a grocery goods undertaking shall not apply dissimilar conditions to equivalent transactions with any other grocery goods undertaking.

(3) Subject to subsection (5), a grocery goods undertaking shall not directly or indirectly compel or coerce, whether by threat, promise or any like means, another grocery goods undertaking to make any payment or grant any allowance for the advertising or display of grocery goods.

(4) Subject to subsection (5) and without limiting the generality of subsection (3), a retailer

A 'grocery goods undertaking' means any undertaking (other than in the restaurant and catering sector) engaged for gain in the production, supply or distribution of food or drink for human consumption. According to section 15B, a grocery goods undertaking shall not directly or indirectly attempt to compel or coerce another grocery goods undertaking. Such coercion may consist of threat, promise or any other means, to resell or advertise for resale any grocery goods at prices fixed directly or indirectly by the first mentioned grocery goods undertaking, or at prices above a minimum price fixed directly or indirectly by the first mentioned grocery goods undertaking. In addition, no coercion should occur aiming at making any payment or granting any allowance for the advertising or display of grocery goods. In addition, a grocery goods undertaking shall not apply dissimilar conditions to equivalent transactions with any other grocery goods undertaking.

G. Slovak Republic

The Slovak legal system contains sector-specific regulations, in the Act on Retail Chains, concerning abuse of economic power which applies only to a purchaser and refers to the conduct of an operator of a retail chain in connection with its supplier in which the retail chain operator abuses a negotiation advantage arising out of its economic power while concluding a contract with the supplier and enforces more advantageous conditions than those it could achieve without such negotiation advantage.[62]

According to paragraph 3:

shall not directly or indirectly compel or coerce, whether by threat, promise or any like means, another grocery goods undertaking to make any payment or grant any allowance to the retailer in consideration of any of the following matters:
(a) providing space for grocery goods within a new retail outlet on or within the first 60 days after its opening to the public;
(b) providing space for grocery goods within a newly expanded or extended retail outlet on or within the first 60 days after the opening to the public of the expanded or extended part of the outlet;
(c) providing space for grocery goods within a retail outlet on or within the first 60 days after its opening to the public under new ownership.
(5) Conduct described in subsections (1) to (4) shall not be prohibited unless it has as its object or effect the prevention, restriction or distortion of competition in trade in any grocery goods in the State or in any part of the State. http://www.tca.ie/EnforcingCompetitionLaw/CompetitionLaw/CompetitionLaw.aspx.

[62] In the Slovak rule of law 'abuse of superior bargaining position' and 'abuse of dominance/monopolization' are assessed pursuant to two autonomous acts. The term abuse of economic power in connection with retail chains is adjusted in the Act No 358/2003 Coll. on Retail Chains in the wording of the Act No 543/2004 Coll. These provisions are enforced by the Ministry of Economy.

(1) Economic power abuse shall be the conduct of an operator of a retail chain in connection with its supplier in which the retail chain operator abuses a negotiation advantage arising out of its economic power within contract conclusion with the supplier and enforces more advantageous conditions than those it could achieve without such negotiation advantage.
(2) An abuse of the economic power shall be in particular:
 a) extortion of inappropriately advantageous business conditions or assertion of discriminatory business conditions during identical or comparable fulfilment towards individual suppliers,
 b) extortion of the obligations in a contract with a supplier not relating to contract subject
 c) forcing the supplier to sell the goods for a price lower than the production or purchase prices,
 d) transfer of sanctions imposed on an operator of a retail chain to a supplier, if they were not imposed by supervision authorities in connection with supplier's responsibility.
(3) Abuse of economic power is contrary to rules of fair business connections 5a) and shall be prohibited.

Thus, in the Slovak Republic, according to paragraph 3(2) an abuse of the economic power is in particular:

a) extortion of inappropriate advantageous business conditions or assertion of discriminatory business conditions during identical or comparable fulfillment towards individual suppliers;
b) extortion of the obligations in a contract with a supplier not relating to contract subject;
c) forcing the supplier to sell the goods for a price lower than the production or purchase prices; and
d) transfer of sanctions imposed on an operator of a retail chain to a supplier, if they were not imposed by supervision authorities in connection with supplier's responsibility.[63]

H. Czech Republic

In the Czech Republic, abuse of superior bargaining position is especially connected with trading chains and their dealing with suppliers. The practices used by trading chains, particularly those of consumers towards suppliers, generally have a civil character (Act No 513/1991 Coll).

[63] ICN Kyoto-ASBP, 20.

As the above analysis illustrates, several EU Member States have clauses in their competition legislation that can address anti-competitive conduct of non-dominant firms.[64] In the jurisdictions analysed above, the concept of abuse of superior bargaining position/abuse of economic dependence applies generally to the whole economy and captures any conduct which may be abusing a superior bargaining position or abusing the economic dependence of an undertaking and causing harm to this undertaking. In some jurisdictions the concept of abuse of economic dependence has a narrow scope of application. Some of these jurisdictions apply the concept only to the buyer side of the market in an attempt to address conduct of large retailers against less powerful suppliers in the conclusion of contracts and other commercial agreements. In some others (eg Ireland) the concept applies only in the grocery sector.

The application of the concept does not vary depending on the size of the economy or for how long a particular jurisdiction has been enforcing competition law. Most of the jurisdictions analysed above use similar criteria to assess abuse of economic dependence and the main point of variation is whether the concept is applied to the buyer side (eg Slovak Republic) or to both the supplier and buyer sides of the market, or whether it applies to particular industries (eg the grocery sector). In most jurisdictions conduct that falls under the concept of abuse of economic dependence relates to exclusionary abuses.[65] The concept of abuse of economic dependence has been applied mainly in relation to anti-competitive conduct towards other firms. The extent to which this concept would capture an exploitative abuse by a non-dominant firm is doubtful. It remains to be seen whether there will be cases that will clarify this grey area of the application of the concept of economic dependence.

I. Concluding Remarks on the Approach of Member States

Article 82 does not address anti-competitive conduct of non-dominant firms and thus leaves a gap in the ability of the Commission to deal with

[64] In addition to the EU Member States, it is worthwhile mentioning Japan. The general competition law in Japan includes a prohibition against unfair trade practices. This prohibition potentially applies to conduct such as unjust refusals to deal, exclusive dealing, restrictive dealing, tie-ins, or charging unjustly low or discriminatory prices. A finding of dominance is not required. The test is whether an undertaking is 'influential in the market'. This is based on factors such as market share (10 per cent or more) and market position (among the top three competitors). Thus, any of the three biggest firms in the market may be considered to be influential in the market and thus may be subject to the law, irrespective of whether it is the biggest firm or not. In order for a conduct by an influential firm to be considered illegal, it must lead to a reduction of the competitors' business opportunities and to making it difficult for them to find alternative trading partners. See further: ICN Kyoto-ASBP, 61.

[65] As noted above, some jurisdictions do not consider the abuse of economic dependence as a competition issue. It is considered a contractual issue.

such conduct, an ability which some Member States possess and use in order to prevent consumer harm from arising from such conduct. For example, the Commission would not be able to deal with Rossignol's anti-competitive conduct in the light of Rossignol's market share of about 8 per cent. The Bundesgerichtshof upheld Rossignol's obligation to supply the sports shop under section 20, paragraph 2 GWB. The Commission would not have been able to be so effective in addressing the consumer harm induced by Rossignol, due to the gap in the application of Article 82.

The abuse of superior bargaining position/abuse of economic dependence is not the only lacuna in the application of Article 82 to anti-competitive unilateral conduct. There is a gap as regards the application of Article 82 to particular conduct of non-dominant firms in general. As was illustrated above, non-dominant firms can have substantial market power due to the differentiation of their products. Such market power can render their conduct harmful to consumers. Capturing such conduct only if the firm is considered to be dominant (giving undue and excessive weight to the market share of the firm) will lead to increased occurrence of Type II errors,[66] not capturing anti-competitive conduct of non-dominant firms. As we will see in the next chapter the likely increased discretion of the Commission to capture conduct of non-dominant firms, will not necessarily lead to an increased number of Type I errors.[67] Rather it should lead to a more effective and accurate application of Article 82 on harmful conduct of firms having the *economic strength ... to prevent effective competition being maintained on the relevant market by affording it the power to behave to an appreciable extent independently of its competitors, customers and ultimately of its consumers.*[68]

[66] 'Type II error' occurs when a conduct which is anti-competitive is not prohibited. We can have Type II errors, inter alia, when harmful conduct of non-dominant firms cannot be captured by the competition legislation. The gap in the application of Article 82 will mainly induce Type II errors but rectifying this gap (by making the definition of the term 'dominant' more dynamic and less dependent on the market share of the allegedly dominant firm) will not only contribute to addressing Type II errors but also Type I errors by enhancin the correct and accurate application of Article 82 on harmful conduct of firms.

[67] 'Type I error' occurs when a conduct which is not anti-competitive is prohibited.

[68] Case 27/76, *United Brands Co. and United Brands Continental BV v Commisison* [1978] ECR I-207, § 65.

CHAPTER 4

The Gap in the Application of Article 82

The concept of the abuse of superior bargaining position relates mainly to contractual relationships between businesses and does not necessarily involve conduct which may be harmful to consumers. However, conduct which harms competitors, may in the long term also harm consumers. The abuse of economic dependence, as it is applied, however, is more related to the relationship between firms rather than the relationship between customers and firms. In addition, the abuse of superior bargaining position in several jurisdictions applies only to the buyer side of the market (eg Latvia, Slovak Republic, Germany). Thus, it applies to conduct by large retailers against suppliers in a worse bargaining position. In the majority of the jurisdictions analysed above, it has not been applied in relation to conduct that the non-dominant supplier may adopt towards customers.

This constitutes a grey area for the applicability of the concept of economic dependence and a second gap in the application of Article 82. In order for an abuse to be exclusionary, it must lead to foreclosure of the market and exit of competitors. In order for such foreclosure to occur, the rivals need to be prevented from accessing customer demand as a result of the anti-competitive conduct of the allegedly abusing non-dominant firm. However, since the market structure in which the gap in the application of Article 82 arises is characterized by differentiation in the products, one of the main premises of the gap argument is that firms do not lose substantial numbers of customers to each other and customers indicate a limited degree of switching between the products of different firms. Thus, since customers are to a certain degree 'captive' in their own preferences towards a particular firm's products, anti-competitive conduct of non-dominant firms are likely to lead to exclusionary abuses, but more importantly to exploitative ones.[1]

[1] The concept of abuse of superior bargaining position applies mainly to conduct of firms against other firms. Cases such as the Rossignol (KZR 1/75, Rossignol, November 20, 1975, WuW/E BGH, 1391) in Germany and the E S against Karelia Tobacco Industry SA case, (Hellenic Competition Commission No 145/11/2000, E S against Karelia Tobacco Industry SA (see further Professor Triantafillakis in I Kokkoris, *Competition Cases from the European Union* (Sweet and Maxwell, London, 2007) in Greece involve the upstream supplier refusing without objective justification to continue its supplies to the downstream supplier (eg imports,

A. Assessment of Dominance

The wording of Article 82 is as follows:

> Any abuse by one or more undertakings of a dominant position within the common market or in a substantial part of it shall be prohibited as incompatible with the common market in so far as it may affect trade between Member States.
>
> Such abuse may, in particular, consist in:
>
> (a) directly or indirectly imposing unfair purchase or selling prices or other unfair trading conditions;
> (b) limiting production, markets or technical development to the prejudice of consumers;
> (c) applying dissimilar conditions to equivalent transactions with other trading parties, thereby placing them at a competitive disadvantage;
> (d) making the conclusion of contracts subject to acceptance by the other parties of supplementary obligations which, by their nature or according to commercial usage, have no connection with the subject of such contracts.

In *Hoffmann-La Roche*[2] the ECJ defined the notion of dominance as 'a position of economic strength enjoyed by an undertaking, which enables it to behave to an appreciable extent independently of its competitors, its customers and ultimately of consumers'.

The ECJ in *United Brands* stated that:

> The dominant position thus referred to (by Article [82]) relates to a position of economic strength enjoyed by an undertaking which enables it to prevent effective competition being maintained on the relevant market by affording it the power to behave to an appreciable extent independently of its competitors, customers and ultimately of its consumers.[3]

As mentioned above, the definition of dominance contains two elements: the ability to prevent effective competition and the ability to behave inde-

distributed goods). For example the upstream firm may limit such supplies in case it is vertically integrated and wishes to foreclose the downstream market to competitors in the downstream market. See also the *Centralcer* case (Procedure 3/98, Portuguese competition authority) where Centralcer abused its position of economic dependence by initiating, in the same area where its exclusive distributors were operating, direct sales to important retailers who had significant market power.

[2] Case 85/76, *Hoffmann-La Roche & Co AG v Commission* [1979] ECR I-461 § 38.

[3] Case 27/76, *United Brands Co and United Brands Continental BV v Commission* [1978] ECR I-207 § 65.

pendently. However, what is unclear is how these two elements relate to each other. From an economic perspective, independent actions do not distinguish between dominant firms and non-dominant firms. No firm can act to an appreciable extent independently of its consumers or customers. This is because each firm is constrained by the demand curve it faces. Firms typically face downward sloping demand curves, indicating that a firm can only charge a higher price if it is willing to make fewer sales. It is not open to the firm to raise prices and sell the same quantity as before. This argument holds both for a dominant and a non-dominant firm.

Four requirements must be met for the application of Article 82. One or more undertakings must be in a dominant position, and such position must be held within the common market or a substantial part of it. In addition, there must be an abuse and this must have an effect on inter-State trade.[4] Dominance is analysed in relation to three variables: the product market, the geographical market and the temporal market.[5] Article 82 does not prohibit the existence of a dominant position, rather it only prohibits its abuse.[6]

The main types of abuse include: excessive pricing[7] (*United Brands*), predatory pricing[8] (*AKZO*[9]); discriminatory pricing[10] (*United Brands*);

[4] A Jones and B Sufrin, *EC Competition Law—Text, Cases and Materials* (2nd edn, OUP, 2004) 255.

[5] P Craig and G De Burc, *EU Law—Text, Cases and Materials* (3rd edition, OUP, 2003) 993.

[6] V Korah, *An Introductory Guide to EC Competition Law and Practice* (5th edn, Oxford, 1994) 83.

[7] On excessive pricing see indicatively: D Elliott, 'What is an Excessive Price?' [2007] 6(8) Comp L I 6(8) 13–15, S Kon, S Turnbull, 'Pricing and the Dominant Firm: Implications of the Competition Commission Appeal Tribunal's Judgment in the Napp case' [2003] 24(2) ECLR 70–86, M Glader, S Larsen(2006) 'Article 82: Excessive Pricing' [2006] 5 (7) Comp L I 3–5, D Geradin, M Rato, 'Excessive Pricing: in Reply' [2006] 5(10) Comp L I 3–5, P Oliver, (2006) 'The Concept of "Abuse" of a Dominant Position under Article 82 EC: Recent Developments in Relation to Pricing' [2006] 1 (2) Euro CJ 315–339.

[8] On predatory pricing see indicatively: M Gal, 'Below-Cost Price Alignment: Meeting or Beating Competition? The France Telecom case' [2007] 28 (6) ECLR 382–391, M Gravengaard, 'The Meeting Competition Defence Principle—a Defence for Price Discrimination and Predatory Pricing?' [2006] 27 (12) CLR 658–677, P Andrews, 'Is Meeting Competition a Defence to Predatory Pricing?—The Irish Sugar Decision Suggests a New Approach' [1998] ECLR 49, T Eilmansberger (2005) 'How to Distinguish Good From Bad Competition Under Article 82 EC: In Search of Clearer and More Coherent Standards for Anti-competitive Abuses' CMLR (PP) 129, OECD, 'Competition Policy Roundtable on Predatory Foreclosure' (15 March 2005) 1–279.

[9] Case C-62/86, *AKZO Chemie BV v Commission* [1991] ECR I-3359.

[10] On price discrimination/rebates see indicatively: OECD, 'Competition Policy Roundtable on Loyalty and Fidelity Discounts and Rebates' (4 March 2003) 1–239, J T Lang, 'Fundamental Issues Concerning Abuse Under Article 82 EC' [2005] Regulatory Policy Institute 19, J T Lang, 'Defining Legitimate Competition: How to Clarify Pricing Abuses Under Article 82' [2002] FILJ 83, M Lorenz, M Lübbig and A Russel (2005), 'Price Discrimination, a Tender Story' [2005] ECLR 355, P Akman, 'To Abuse, or Not to Abuse: Discrimination between Consumers' [2007] 32 (4) E L Rev 492–512, D Gerard, (2005) 'Price

refusal to supply[11] (*Commercial Solvents*[12]); tying in[13] (*Hilti*,[14] *Tetra Pak II*[15]); loyalty rebates (*Hoffman-La Roche*); abuse of intellectual property rights (*Magill*[16]); and vexatious litigation (*Promedia*[17]). As the judgment in *Continental Can*[18] clarified, though, Article 82 did not set out an exhaus-

Discrimination under Article 82(c) EC: Clearing up the Ambiguities' in (July) Global Competition Law Centre Research Papers on Article 82 EC 133, J T Lang and R O'Donoghue (2002) 'Defining Legitimate Competition: How to Clarify Pricing Abuses under Article 82EC' [2002] 26 Fordham International Law Journal 83, M Armstrong and J Vicker, 'Price Discrimination, Competition and Regulation' [1993] 41 Journal of Industrial Economics 335, A Perrot, 'Towards an Effects-based Approach of Price Discrimination' in *The Pros and Cons of Price Discrimination* (Swedish Competition Authority, 2005), D Ridyard, 'Exclusionary Pricing and Price Discrimination Abuses under Article 82—An Economic Analysis' [2002] 6 ECLR 286, M Armstrong, 'Recent Developments in the Economics of Price Discrimination' October 2005 Working Paper, http://129.3.20.41/eps/io/papers/0511/0511004.pdf, R Schmalensee, 'Output and Welfare Implications of Monopolistic Third-Degree Price Discrimination' [1981] 71 The American Economic Review 242, H R Varian, 'Price Discrimination and Social Welfare' [1985] 75 The American Economic Review 870, P Muysert, 'Price Discrimination—An Unreliable Indicator of Market Power' [2004] 6 ECLR 350.

[11] On refusal to deal/essential facilities see indicatively: C Nagy, 'Refusal to deal and the doctrine of essential facilities in US and EC competition law: a comparative perspective and a proposal for a workable analytical framework' [2007] 32(5) E L Rev 664–685, D Carlton, 'A General Analysis of Exlusionary Conduct and Refusal to Deal—Why Aspen and Kodak Are Misguided', NBER Working Paper No 8105 (2001), www.nber.org/papers/w8105, Z Chen, T Ross & W T Stanbury, 'Refusals to Deal and Aftermarkets' [1998] 13 Review of Industrial Organization 131, B Doherty, 'Just What Are Essential Facilities?' [2001] 38 CMLR 397, A Jones, 'A Dominant Firm's Duty to Deal: EC and US Antitrust Law Compared' in *Handbook of Research in Transatlantic Antitrust* (Philip Marsden (ed) 2006), J T Lang, 'Defining Legitimate Competition: Companies' Duties to Supply Competitors and Access to Essential Facilities' [1994] 18 Fordham International Law Journal 437, M Lao, 'Aspen Skiing and Trinko: Antitrust Intent and Sacrifice' [2005] 73 Antitrust Law Journal 171, OECD, 'The Essential Facilities Concept' Background Note, OCDE/GD(96)113, G Robinson, 'On Refusing to Deal with Rivals' [2002] 87 Cornell Law Review 1177, A Stratakis, 'Comparative Analysis of the US and EU Approach and Enforecement of the Essential Facilities Doctrine' [2006] 27 ECLR 434, J Venit, 'Article 82: The Last Frontier—Fighting Fire with Fire?' [2005] 28 Fordham International Law Journal 1157.

[12] Cases 6&7/73, *Instituto Chemioterapico Italiano SpA and Commercial Solvents Corp v Commission (Commercial Solvents)* [1974] ECR 223.

[13] On tying and bundling see indicatively: D Spector, 'From Harm to Competitors to Harm to Competition: One More Effort, Please!' [2006] 2(1) Euro CJ Supp (Special issue) 145–162, K-U Kuhn, R Stillman, C Caffarra (2005) 'Economic Theories of Bundling and their Policy Implications in Abuse Cases: an Assessment in Light of the Microsoft Case' [2005] 1(1) Euro CJ 85–121, D Ridyard, 'Tying and Bundling—Cause for Complaint?' [2005] 26 (6) ECLR 316–319, M Furse, 'Article 82, Microsoft and bundling, or "The Half Monti"' [2004] 3(3) Comp LJ 169–178, JTirole, 'The Analysis of Tying Cases: A Primer' [2005] 1 Comp Policy Int'l 1, Bellamy & Child, *European Community Law of Competition* (6th edn, OUP, 2008) para 10.119–10.120, Bishop and Walker, *The Economics of EC Competition Law* (2nd edn, Sweet and Maxwell, 2002) 209, Nalebuff, *Bundling, Tying and Portfolio Effects*, DTI Economics Paper No 1, February 2003, E Iacobucci, *Tying as quality control: A legal and economic analysis, University of Toronto*, Faculty of Law, Law and Economics. Research Paper No 01-09, http://papers.ssrn.com/abstract=293602, W S Bowman, 'Tying Arrangements and the Leverage Problem', 67 Yale L.R.19 (19–36) (1957), Hylton and Salinger, 'Tying Law and Policy: A Decision-Theoretic Approach [2001] 69 Antitrust LJ 469 (486), C Ahlborn and D S Evans and A J Padilla, 'The Antitrust Economics of Tying: a Farewell to Per Se Illegality', The Antitrust Bulletin/Spring–Summer 2004, 287 (323), D W Carlton & Michael Waldman,

tive enumeration of the types of abuses of a dominant position prohibited by the EC Treaty.[19]

In a market with differentiated products each of the firms has a degree of independence from its competitors. As we will analyse in this section, this product differentiation allows the second biggest firm in the market to adopt anti-competitive conduct harming consumer welfare. The structural approach towards the definition of the concept of dominance, does not allow the Commission to tackle such conduct.

As regards the assessment of dominance, for dominance to exist the undertaking(s) concerned must not be subject to active competitive constraints. In other words, it must have substantial market power. It is also not required for a finding of dominance that the undertaking in question has eliminated all opportunity for competition on the market. For Article 82 to apply it is not a condition that competition has been eliminated. In conducting the analysis of whether the allegedly dominant undertaking 'has the power to behave to an appreciable extent independently of its competitors, its customers and ultimately of the consumers', it is relevant to consider in particular the market position of the allegedly dominant undertaking, the market position of competitors, barriers to expansion and entry, and the market position of buyers.[20]

The existence of a dominant position may derive from several factors which, taken separately, are not necessarily determinative. According to the

'The Strategic Use of Tying to Preserve and Create Market Power in Evolving Industries' [2002] 33 Rand J Econ 194, JCarbajo, D de Meza, D J Seidmann, 'A Strategic Motivation for Commodity Bundling [1990] 38 The Journal of Industrial Economics 283, D J Seidmann, 'Bundling as a Facilitating Device: A Reinterpretation of Leverage Theory' [1991] 58 Economica 491, Y Chen, 'Equilibrium Product Bundling' [1997] 70 J Bus 85, R P McAfee, J McMillan and M D Whinston, 'Multiproduct Monopoly, Commodity Bundling and Correlation of Values [1989] 104 Q J Econ 371, W J Adams & J L Yellen, 'Commodity Bundling and the Burden of Monopoly' [1976] 90 Q J Econ 475, R L Schmalensee, 'Gaussian Demand and Commodity Bundling' [1984] 57 J Bus 211, M A Salinger, 'A Graphical Analysis of Bundling' [1995] 68 J Bus 85, K N Hylton & M Salinger, 'Tying Law and Policy: A Decision—Theoritic Approach [2001] 69 Antitrust Law Journal 469 (470–71), K-U Kühn, R Stillman, C Caffarra, *Economic Theories of Bundling and Their Policy Implication in Abuse Cases: An Assessment in Light of the Microsoft Case*, CEPR Discussion Paper No 4756 (2005), T A Lampert, *Evaluating Bundled Discounts*, 89 Minn L Rev 1688, 1700–1705 (2004–2005), D A Crane, 'Multiproduct Discounting: A Myth of Nonprice Predation [2005] 72 U Chi L Rev 27.

14 Case T-30/89, *Hilti v Commission* [1991] ECR II-1439, confirmed C-53/92P, [1994] ECR I-666.

15 Case T-83/91, *Tetra Pak Rausing SA v Commission (Tetra Pak II)* [1994] ECR II-755.

16 *Magill TV Guide* [1989] OJ L78/43.

17 Case T-111/96, *ITT Promedia NV v Commission (Promedia)* [1998] ECR II-2937.

18 Case 72/71 *Re Continental Can Co Inc* [1972] OJ L7/25.

19 See further: *Europemballage Corp and Continental Can Co Inc v Commission (Continental Can)* [1973] ECR I-215, §26.

20 Annex 2 presents a table (taken from the ICN Report) of the most important criteria that countries use to assess single firm dominance/substantial market power.

Economic Advisory Group, traditional means of establishing dominance through information about market structure are proxies for the determination of dominance; they assess the ability to exert power and impose abusive behaviour on other market participants.[21]

The factors that need to be present for dominance, inter alia, include:

- large market shares;
- no close competitors;
- customers have limited possibilities of switching supplier;
- competitors are capacity constrained;
- firm is able to hinder expansion by competitors.

All respondents to the ICN questionnaire for the ICN Report stated that they use a comprehensive set of criteria to assess dominance and generally consider market share and barriers to entry or expansion and durability of market power as the most important criteria. Market shares are used as an initial indicator or starting point for the market power analysis. Over half of the agency respondents note that their jurisdictions use market share thresholds as a rebuttable presumption of dominance and/or a safe harbour.[22]

The following list provides an overview of the assessment factors in order of their importance:

- market share of the firm and its competitors;
- market position and market behavior of competitors;
- barriers to entry or expansion;
- buyer power;
- economies of scale and scope/network effects;
- access to upstream markets/vertical integration;
- durability of market power;
- market maturity/vitality;
- access to essential facilities;
- financial resources of the firm and its competitors;
- high prices (at absolute or comparative level);
- profits of the firm.

Market shares provide useful first indications of the market structure and of the competitive importance of various undertakings active on the market. Many ICN jurisdictions have some form of market-share-based presumption

[21] EAGCP Report 14.

[22] See Annex 2 of this book. Annex 2 presents a table (taken from the ICN Report) of the most important criteria that countries use to assess single firm dominance/substantial market power.

of dominance. Such presumptions may lead to increased enforcement efficiency and legal certainty. Jurisdictions have presumptions of different sorts and employ varying market share levels for their presumptions.

The Commission interprets market shares in the light of likely market conditions, for instance, whether the market is highly dynamic in character and whether the market structure is unstable due to innovation or growth. The benefits of using market shares as a first indication must be weighed against the risks, in particular potential over-emphasis on market shares and thus potential enforcement errors.

The Commission in the Discussion paper states that:

> It is very likely that very high markets shares, which have been held for some time, indicate a dominant position. This would be the case where an undertaking holds 50 per cent or more of the market, provided that rivals hold a much smaller share of the market. In the case of lower market shares, dominance is more likely to be found in the market share range of 40 per cent to 50 per cent than below 40 per cent, although also undertakings with market shares below 40 per cent could be considered to be in a dominant position. However, undertakings with market shares of no more than 25 per cent are not likely to enjoy a (single) dominant position on the market concerned.[23]

Monti argues that this passage indicates the Commission's ability to apply Article 82 to conduct of firms having low market shares.[24] Monti further argues that the legal passages[25] that the Commission refers to in the Discussion Paper imply that dominance is as likely to be found with market shares below 40 per cent as it is to be found with higher market shares.[26]

The lowest market share which substantiated a finding of dominance is just under 40 per cent in *BA/Virgin*.[27] The Commission and the courts have

[23] The Commission in the Guidance Paper argues that there may be specific cases below that threshold where competitors are not in a position to constrain effectively the conduct of a dominant undertaking, for example where they face serious capacity limitations. In such cases the Commission may also investigate anticompetitive conducts. Although the Commission makes an attempt to apply Article 82 on firms having low market shares which are able though to adopt anticompetitive conducts, it does not liberate the analysis from the factor of dominance. Thus, non-dominant firms having low market shares in differentiated product markets or in markets where capacity constraints are significant, can still adopt anticompetitive conducts and harm consumer welfare. § 31.

[24] G Monti, 'The Concept of Dominance in Article 82', [2006] European Competition Journal 31–52, 50.

[25] *Gøttrup-Klim ea Grovvareforeninger v Dansk Landbrugs Grovvareselskab AmbA* C-250/92 [1994] ECR I-5641, *United Brands v European Commission* C-27/76, [1978] ECR -207.

[26] G Monti, 'The Concept of Dominance in Article 82' [2006] European Competition Journal 31–52, page 50.

[27] *BA/Virgin* [2000] OJ L 30/1.

never alleged that a firm having the second highest market share in a market can be dominant and thus that this firm abuses its dominance by adopting anti-competitive conduct.

The practice of the Commission and the courts illustrate dependence of the concept of dominance on the market shares of the allegedly dominant firms. There is no case, to the author's knowledge, where it has been alleged that the second biggest firm is 'dominant' or 'abuses its dominant position'.

The Commission 'in theory' (ie in the Guidance Paper, etc), argues that market share is a first indication and is not conclusive evidence of a firm's dominant position. However, the relative market shares of the firms in a market seem to constitute a safe harbour, ie if the second biggest firm has a market share close to the allegedly dominant firm's, it is unlikely that the Commission and courts will ever argue that the highest market share firm is dominant. Similarly, the Commission and courts will not argue that the second biggest firm is dominant.

As was shown above, the Commission's decisions and the CFI/ECJ judgments imply that Article 82 has a consumer welfare objective. Thus, Article 82 is enforced in order to safeguard consumer welfare. The gap in the application of Article 82 arises in all situations where the two biggest firms have close market shares, their products are differentiated and, although the biggest firm's conduct would be considered abusive, the second biggest firm's conduct would not.

Under the assumption that the objective of Article 82 is consumer welfare, we can argue that a firm which is dominant because it has 45 per cent of the market by adopting an anti-competitive conduct abuses its dominant position, and harms a significant number of customers.[28] However, we cannot argue that the second biggest firm which has 40 per cent of the market is dominant and thus, cannot prevent it under Article 82, from adopting an anti-competitive conduct, similar to the one that the biggest firm adopted. This inability of Article 82 to be applied to firms having significant (but not the highest) market share is counterintuitive, since Article 82 has a consumer welfare objective and the second firm's conduct may harm a similar number of customers as the biggest firm's conduct.[29]

[28] The market shares used in this paragraph are indicative. An assumption is made that the other factors that would indicate dominance are present (eg high barriers to entry, capacity constraints etc). Depending, inter alia, on the differentiation of the products, the existence of alternative, as well as the switching costs of consumers and the capacity utilization of the rivals, the dominant firm's (accounting for the 45 per cent market share) anti-competitive conduct may harm a significant proportion of customers.

[29] The premise behind this book and the theory analysed herein are that the second biggest firm is not significantly smaller than the biggest firm and that the other criteria that would render a firm dominant in a market are present (eg barriers to entry, lack of buyer power etc). The differentiation of the products makes any likelihood of collective dominance remote. See

Although reference throughout this book is made to the second biggest firm in the market, the same arguments can be made for the firms with similar market shares in a differentiated products market. Thus, if the third biggest firm's market share is similar to the top two, the same arguments as regards the consumer harm induced by adopting possible anti-competitive conduct can be made. Not all non-dominant firms can be liable for inducing consumer harm. This gap will normally refer to the conduct by a non-dominant firm with a market share close to the biggest firm's market share in the market. It may also refer to the third biggest firm in the market when it is of similar size to the two bigger firms. Thus, this book does not argue that any anti-competitive conduct by any non-dominant firm should be subject to scrutiny under Article 82; only the conduct of these non-dominant firms which is likely to induce significant consumer harm, a harm that had it been induced by the dominant firm, would have been scrutinized under Article 82.

As the Economic Advisory Group argued, the assessment of competitive harm must be based on an assessment of how competition in the particular market works and what the practice in question means for market participants. The standard for assessing whether a given practice is detrimental to competition or whether it is a legitimate tool of competition should be derived from the effects of the practice on consumers. How then can the consumer welfare objective of Article 82 be reconciled with the fact a firm's conduct which may harm 40 per cent of the market is not caught by Article 82?

We should make at this stage one important observation. In order for a firm to be considered to be dominant, having a market share close to the second biggest firm, there are some assumptions that need to be satisfied as regards the market structure. One very important element is product differentiation. Products may differ in the eyes of customers, for instance due to brand image, product features, product quality, a full line of goods or services, complete systems, level of service, or the location of the seller. When products are differentiated, those customers who like a particular brand's attributes are likely to continue to purchase that brand even after the producer increases its prices.[30] In such a situation, the products are not fully substitutable in the eyes of the customers but they still constitute one antitrust market. There are quite a few merger cases in which there are highly differentiated products, but they belong to a wider antitrust market.[31]

further: I Kokkoris, 'The Development of the Concept of Collective Dominance in the European Community Merger Regulation from its Inception to its Current Status' (2007) World Competition.

30 The increase in the price is only one example of consumer harm induced by a firm which exploits its substantial market power.

31 See eg software products in *Oracle/Peoplesoft* (Case M3216 *Oracle/PeopleSoft* [2005]

In addition to the implications that product differentiation has for the ability and incentive of non-dominant firms to adopt anti-competitive conduct, firms may have the incentive to adopt such conduct due to 'supply side' features of the market. Markets with a similar structure can display different degrees of intra-market rivalry as a result of many factors. Non-structural factors that might affect the level of intra-market rivalry can include, for example, the different ability of, and capacity for, firms to innovate; the objectives and culture of the firms in the market, their views on the future development of the market and on the appropriate strategies to meet those developments; the history of pricing behaviour in the market and the extent to which transparent prices are available in the market.[32]

Thus, there are a number of other structural factors beyond market share/market concentration and product differentiation that can affect the degree of intra-market rivalry in a market. For instance, the extent of intra-market rivalry may depend on whether firms' cost structures are very similar or not, and how low-cost firms utilize this advantage. In addition, the degree of spare capacity in a market and the ease with which existing capacity can be expanded are two factors that might impinge on the degree of intra-market rivalry. These factors which induce different degrees of intra-market rivalry in the presence of differentiated products may bestow the incentives to the incumbents and confer on them the ability to unilaterally adopt anti-competitive conduct without the fear of losing significant market share.

B. Implications of Differentiation

Product differentiation refers to such variations within a product class that (some) consumers view as imperfect substitutes. Products are differentiated in the perception of consumers. There are many different goods, each of

OJ L218/6), music recordings in *Sony/BMG* (Case M3333 *Sony/BMG* [2005] OJ L62/30). Most retail markets are likely to involve differentiated products. With highly differentiated consumer products, the relevant market delineated by the hypothetical monopolist paradigm may be as narrow as two products. G Werden, L Froeb, 'Calibrated Economic Models Add Focus, Accuracy, and Persuasiveness to Merger Analysis' (2002) www2.owen.vanderbilt.edu/luke.froeb/papers/sca10.pdf 13. For further background on product differentiation see indicatively R Brenkers, F Verboven (2005) 'Market Definition with Differentiated Products—Lessons from the Car Market', http://www.cepr.org/pubs/dps/DP5249.asp, A Nevo, 'Mergers with Differentiated Products: The Case of Ready-to-Eat Cereal', Competition Policy Center, Paper CPC99-002 (1997) http://repositories.cdlib.org/iber/cpc/CPC99-002, K Shapiro (1996), 'Mergers with Differentiated Products' [1996] Antitrust http://www.usdoj.gov/atr/public/speeches/shapiro.spc.htm, A Majumdar, 'The Role of A Consumer Harm Test in Competition Policy', Draft for Discussion (2007) http://64.233.169.104/search?q=cache:7X1vk0Kcns4J:www.luc.edu/law/academics/special/center/antitrust/pdfs/consumer_harm.pdf+differentiated+products+markets+in+competition+policy&hl=en&ct=clnk&cd=90&gl=us.

32 *Market Investigation References: Competition Commission Guidelines*, www.competition-commission.org.uk.

which exists in a number of forms or variants. The differentiation of products can be vertical or horizontal, ie each product may exist in a number of qualities or in a number of variants of equal quality.[33]

In the *United Brands* case, the ECJ argued that one significant factor indicating dominance was United Brands' brand image. United Brand had spent significant resources establishing the brand. Furthermore, the ECJ considered that United Brands had made their product distinctive by using large-scale advertising and promotion which had induced the consumer to show a preference for it in spite of the difference between the price of labelled and unlabelled bananas and thus had made its brand name the premier banana brand name.[34] Thus, the ECJ placed emphasis on the differentiated nature of the product emanating from the brand image of the product.

In the theory of industrial organization, two models that describe the nature of competition in a market are the Cournot and the Bertrand models.[35] A distinction can be made between markets where firms compete primarily in output/capacity and markets where firms compete primarily in prices. The first type of market structure resembles Cournot oligopoly; the second resembles Bertrand oligopoly. The Cournot model of oligopoly assumes that firms produce homogeneous products and compete by setting output to maximize profits and takes the output of other firms as fixed. The Bertrand model of oligopoly assumes that firms set price in order to maximise profits and takes as given the prices of other firms in the market.

In the Cournot model of competition, firms compete by setting quantities and thus firms' quantities are substitutes. A reduction in the output of the firm producing homogeneous products typically leads competing firms

[33] Articles on product differentiation include, inter alia: J Baker and T Bresnahan, 'The Gains from Merger or Collusion in Product Differentiated Industries' [1985] Journal of Industrial Economics 33, 427–444. A Dixit, 'A Model of Duopoly Suggesting a Theory of Entry Barriers' [1979] Bell Journal of Economics 10, 20–32; J Hausman, 'A Proposed Method for Analysing Competition among Differentiated Products', [1992] Antitrust Law Journal 60, 889–900; C Shapiro, 'Mergers with Differentiated Products' [1996] Antitrust 10, 23–30; N Singh and X Vives, 'Price and Quantity Competition in a Differentiated Duopoly' [1984] Rand Journal of Economics 15, 546–554; G Werden, 'A Robust Test for Consumer Welfare Enhancing Mergers among Sellers of Differentiated Products' [1982] Journal of Industrial Economics 44, 409–414; H Hotelling, 'Stability in Competition' [1929] Economic Journal 39, 41–57; A Irmen, J F Thisse, 'Competition in Multi-Characteristics Spaces: Hotelling Was Almost Right' [1998] Journal of Economic Theory 76–102, 78; M Mussa, S Rosen, 'Monopoly and Product Quality' [1978] 18 Journal of Economic Theory 301–317; A Shaked, J Sutton (1982), 'Relaxing Price Competition through Product Differentiation' [1982] Review of Economic Studies 49, 3–14.

[34] Case 27/76 *United Brands Company and United Brands Continental BV v Commission of the European Communities* [1978] ECR 207 § 91, 93 and 122–124.

[35] In 1838 Antoine Augustin Cournot published the first systematic analysis of oligopoly, arguing that firms compete by setting quantities. In 1883, Joseph Louis Francois Bertrand in reviewing Cournot's book argued that competitors compete by setting their prices.

to expand their own output, although not to the extent of fully compensating the initial output reduction.[36] Hence, anti-competitive conduct by a non-dominant firm may not necessarily lead to significant consumer harm, since the decrease in the output by this firm will be compensated by the increase in output from the incumbent firms in the market.

In the Bertrand model of competition, firms will converge upon the equilibrium price and quantity whether products are homogeneous (to the price that would prevail in a perfectly competitive market) or differentiated[37] (to prices above to the price that would prevail in a perfectly competitive market). With product differentiation, firms are able to adjust prices without losing the entire market. In such cases, prices do not rapidly collapse to marginal cost (as would be the case under perfect competition) and hence the adoption of anti-competitive conduct by a non-dominant firm is profitable for all the firms in the market. The adverse impact of such conduct on competition in the market may be substantial, even if the differentiated products of the incumbent firms are not close substitutes.

When firms compete in prices (eg Bertrand model) these prices are often complements. This implies that an increase in the price of one good will typically lead competing firms to increase their prices, although probably to a lesser extent. An increase in a firm's prices triggers a positive response from the other firms, thereby further encouraging this firm to raise its own prices. Because of the complementarity of the prices, the direct impact of this conduct on the market is exacerbated by the rival firms' adaptation. Thus, more generally the adoption of any anti-competitive conduct by a non-dominant firm is likely to induce significant consumer harm, since the rival firms will not be able to fully countervail the consumer harm induced by this conduct. If the non-dominant firm has a substantial market share in the market, albeit not the highest, the induced consumer harm is likely to be very significant.

It should be noted that large profit margins can be observed as a result of conduct having an adverse impact on competition as well as in industries with differentiated products in which the products of different firms are not close substitutes. In a differentiated product market, firms are able to adjust prices without losing the entire market. In such cases, prices do not rapidly

[36] Provided there are no capacity constraints. In the presence of capacity constraints unless new entry can occur within a reasonable period of time, rivals cannot counteract the decrease in the output of the firm. What constitutes an appropriate time period depends on the characteristics and dynamics of the market, as well as on the specific capabilities of potential entrants. The Commission in its Horizontal Merger Guidelines, entry is normally only considered timely if it occurs within two years. (*Guidelines on the assessment of horizontal mergers under the Council Regulation on the control of concentrations between undertakings*, OJ C 31, 05.02.2004, 5–18, paragraph 74)

[37] The significance of product differentiation may be diminished if it is possible for competitors to reposition their products to compete directly with the non-dominant firm's products, (eg by engaging in brand repositioning or introducing new brands).

collapse to marginal cost (as would be the case under perfect competition) and hence the adoption of anti-competitive conduct is profitable for the non-dominant firm.

When firms sell differentiated products, each firm faces a downward sloping demand curve. This is because if it raises its price above the price that its competitors are charging, it does not lose all of its customers, because some of them are willing to pay more for the special features of that particular differentiated product.

For industries with either differentiated or undifferentiated goods the inverse demand curve[38] facing firm A is:

$$p_A = D(q_1 \dots q_n)$$

p_A is the price that firm A will charge which will depend on the quantity of its own brands as well as of the other brands $q_1 \dots q_n$ sold.

For simplicity, assume that firm A's demand curve in a market with two brands of a product is:

$$p_A = a - b_A q_A - b_B q_B$$

where the absolute value of b_A is higher than the one of b_B. An increase in firm A's output has a greater impact on its price than an increase in firm B's output. Thus, the more differentiated brand A is the more impervious to the actions of the competitors is firm A. The more differentiated the product, the higher and more inelastic is the demand that firm A faces, and thus the more able it is to increase prices and adopt other anti-competitive conduct without the fear of losing substantial market share. Market power, measured in terms of the price-cost margin, is positively related to quality and to horizontal product differentiation.

Competitive pressure is likely to be weak (and thus firms are likely to have market power) the smaller the number of firms interacting strategically, the smaller the degree of substitutability between products is small (thus products are significantly horizontally differentiated) and the larger the quality advantage of the firm's products (thus products are significantly vertically differentiated).[39]

The actual degree of market power, measured in terms of price-cost margins, decreases in the number of firms that interact strategically and in the average quality level of the competitors, and increases in the firm's product quality level, as well as in the degree of horizontal differentiation.

[38] Inverse demand curve is the normal demand curve solved for the price.

[39] J Häckner (1999), 'Market Delineation and Product Differentiation' http://www.ne.su.se/paper/wp99_07.pdf.

The Discussion Paper acknowledges the significance of differentiation (more than the Guidance paper does) and states that the importance of market shares may be qualified by an analysis of the degree of product differentiation in the market. When products are differentiated the competitive constraint that they impose on each other is likely to differ even where they form part of the same relevant market.

As the Commission adds in the Discussion Paper:

> Substitutability is a question of degree. In assessing the competitive constraint imposed by rivals, it must therefore be taken into account what is the degree of substitutability of their products with those offered by the allegedly dominant undertaking. It may be that a rival with 10 per cent market share imposes a greater competitive constraint on an undertaking with 50 per cent market share than another rival supplying 20 per cent of the market. This may for instance be the case where the undertaking with the lower market share and the allegedly dominant undertaking both sell premium branded products whereas the rival with the larger market share sells a bargain brand.[40]

What should be taken into account in differentiated product markets where firms produce substitute products is the diversion ratio,[41] which will indicate the diversion of sales from the products of one firm to those of the other firm, in case of anti-competitive conduct by that firm. This diversion ratio is calculated by looking at customers' choices if they switch away from a firm that adopts the anti-competitive conduct (eg increases its price). If the products are differentiated, so that products sold by different participants in the market are not perfect substitutes for one another, an anti-competitive conduct by the second biggest firm in a market with differentiated products may diminish competition by enabling it to profit by this conduct, without at the same time incurring substantial switching of customers from its products to its rivals' products.

In addition, the degree of profitability of the adoption of anti-competitive conduct will depend on the elasticity of the product involved. If the product is highly elastic then the adoption of anti-competitive conduct will divert sales to substitute products and therefore significantly affect profits. Such a result will of course depend on the extent to which substitute products exist and can be offered to consumers. If the firms producing substitute products face capacity constraints such as significant costs or time

[40] § 33.

[41] The closeness of substitution between products does not only depend on the degree of differentiation of these products, but also on factors such as capacity constraints and barriers to entry and expansion.

constraints, or where entry into the market of new players with substitute products is difficult, then the adoption of anti-competitive conduct by the incumbent firm is likely to be very profitable.

In the presence of capacity constraints we can envisage a homogenous market where the non-dominant firm will adopt abusive conduct, and the rivals will not be able to mitigate the impact of the non-dominant firm's conduct. So not only the dominant firm but the other incumbents as well may be unable to countervail the anti-competitive conduct of the non-dominant firm. Such conduct in markets which are characterized by general capacity constraints will lead to the same anti-competitive outcomes as the conduct of non-dominant firms in differentiated markets in the absence of capacity constraints.

The analysis herein will mainly focus on differentiated markets, since in homogenous markets characterized by capacity constraints, in the absence of significant barriers to entry, entrants may mitigate the anti-competitive impact of abusive conduct of non-dominant firms. In contrast, such entry may not fully mitigate non-dominant firms' abusive conduct in differentiated markets. We should emphasize, though, that the implications of the analysis herein apply in both abovementioned situations. The anti-competitive conduct of non-dominant firms in both these market situations needs to be addressed by the authorities.

Similarly, in the presence of significant switching costs (eg inconvenience, monetary costs, administrative hurdles or a lack of information about the products of alternative suppliers), even in homogeneous markets, the customers will not likely switch to other rivals, bestowing thus the non-dominant firm with market power and with the ability to adopt anti-competitive conduct. Where customers face difficulties in switching between suppliers, whether because of the monetary costs, administrative hurdles or inconvenience, competition can be affected due to a reduction in the rivalry between firms. Switching costs allow firms potentially to charge high prices to customers that are unlikely to switch. Firms may engage in practices that increase switching costs, for example, by not releasing information needed for a switch to be feasible or by not doing so in a timely fashion, endorsing loyalty cards.

The implication of differentiation in the firms' products is focusing on the limited customer switching that this product differentiation induces. Differentiation in the products induces inertia in customers. Thus, in the analysis throughout this book we will refer to the issue of differentiated products as a precondition for anti-competitive conduct of non-dominant firms, but we will be also incorporating the possibility and the induced implications of significant customer inertia for non-dominant firms' anti-competitive conduct due to factors other than the differentiated nature of the product. This inertia arises due to switching costs that customers may face.

Capacity constraints play an important role in the ability of rivals to mitigate anti-competitive conduct by a non-dominant firm. In the case of a market with differentiated products, capacity constraints are not so important, as in markets with homogeneous products, since the output of the firms (and their reaction to each other's strategies) is unlikely to change much in the presence of anti-competitive conduct by the second biggest in the market, in contrast to the case of the Cournot type of competition, where, since the products are homogeneous, inability of the rival firms (eg the dominant firm) to increase their capacity may lead the second biggest firm, as analysed above, to adopt anti-competitive conduct.

When products are differentiated, those customers who like a particular brand's attributes are likely to continue to purchase that brand even after the firm adopts a certain anti-competitive conduct. Thus, the incentives of a firm to switch in the presence of such conduct are low and in turn the firm's incentives to adopt such conduct are more significant compared to the situation of homogeneous products, where the switching of customers is likely to be much more intense.[42] Thus, if the second biggest firm in a market adopts anti-competitive conduct, its actions are not constrained by the presence of a firm with larger market share. Although some of the non-dominant firm's customers will switch, the number of customers who will switch will not be significant enough to prevent the non-dominant firm from adopting anti-competitive conduct. For example, non-dominant firms can price-discriminate against their customers without fear of losing a significant portion of their demand. We should emphasize that this anti-competitive conduct of the non-dominant firm cannot be addressed by Article 82.

We can see a graphical representation of this switching in the following graph.

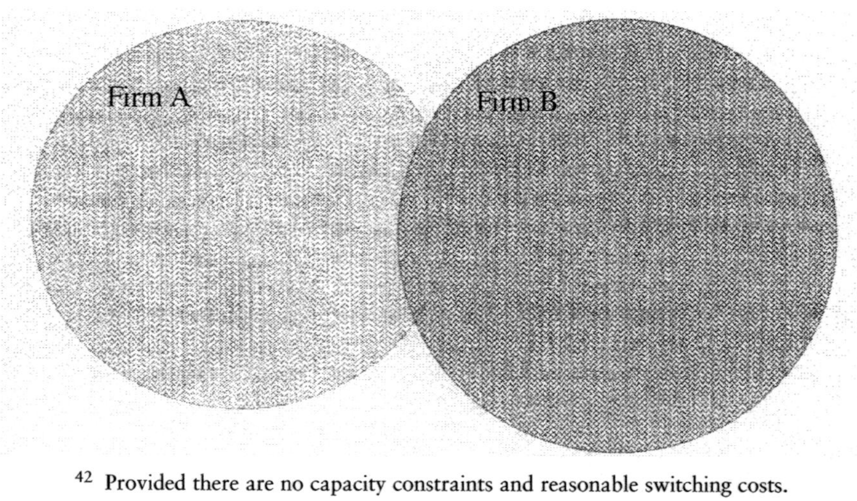

[42] Provided there are no capacity constraints and reasonable switching costs.

If we assume that the two circles represent the customer groups (and respective market shares) of the products of two firms producing differentiated products, the adoption of anti-competitive conduct by one of the firms will lead to the switching of the customers in the overlapping area. This limited switching will not provide the incentive to the firms to avoid adopting such conduct. In the case of homogenous products, the number of customers switching would be much greater, since customers are likely to consider these homogeneous products more substitutable for each other than would be the case if the products were different.

If firm A adopts anti-competitive conduct, since it is the second biggest firm in the market, the Commission will not be able to penalize this conduct as firm A will not be considered to be dominant. If, on the other hand, firm B adopts the same conduct, the Commission is able to allege that this firm is dominant[43] and thus penalize it, while in reality the actual difference in the harm to consumer welfare is small compared to the consumer welfare harm induced by Firm A's conduct. Thus, if Article 82's objective is consumer welfare, the Commission should be able to apply Article 82 in the case of anti-competitive conduct that firm A adopts.

C. The Gap

Under EU competition law, it is long established in case law that dominant undertakings have a 'special' obligation to avoid behaviour which can restrain, distort or hinder competition.[44] However, Temple Lang[45] argues that this special obligation simply means that Article 82 applies to dominant undertakings. It means that conduct which is perfectly lawful for ordinary (non-dominant) undertakings may be unlawful if it is carried out by a dominant undertaking.[46] The non-dominant firm, however defined, is not subject to the restraints of Article 82, so that it is free from restraints on the choice of business practices which bind its larger rivals. In adopting its own business plan, a non-dominant firm will not routinely or willingly adopt strategies on pricing, bundling, tie-ins, or rebates that make its operations

[43] Notwithstanding the similar market shares, in a differentiated product market, each firm's market power is not equivalent to its market share, since the limited switching is likely to make this firm more independent in its actions. As the Commission mentioned in the Discussion Paper, it may be that a rival with 10 per cent market share imposes a greater competitive constraint on an undertaking with 50 per cent market share than another rival supplying 20 per cent of the market. This may for instance be the case where the undertaking with the lower market share and the allegedly dominant undertaking both sell premium branded products whereas the rival with the larger market share sells a bargain brand.

[44] eg Case 322/81, *Michelin v Commission* [1983] ECR 3461.

[45] Temple Lang, 'European Competition Law and Compulsory Licensing of Intellectual Property Rights—a Comprehensive Principle' [2004] 4 Europarättslig Tidskrift 558–588.

[46] B Vesterdorf, 'Article 82 EC: Where do we stand after the Microsoft judgement?' http://www.icc.qmul.ac.uk/GAR/Vesterdorf.pdf.

inefficient. Anti-competitive practices by non-dominant firms illustrate the inability of the European Commission to address the competitive harm induced by this conduct.

The OECD in its policy brief on *Substantial Market Power and Competition*[47] argued that there is substantial agreement that single firm conduct provisions should apply only to firms with a high degree of market power. Unilateral acts by a firm with a high degree of market power are much more likely to harm consumer welfare and distort the competitive process than are unilateral act by firms with little or no power. The OECD adds that there is no single, clear economic test that can be used to distinguish between market power that is of concern in unilateral conduct cases and the lesser degree of market power that should not be. It all depends on the ability of undertakings to adversely influence competition. Thus, it is clear that non-dominant firms can also have an adverse impact on consumer welfare by adopting unilateral acts.

The importance of the dominance test lies in the fact that a screening based on a legal concept similar to the economic notion of market power prevents the prohibition of pro-competitive unilateral practices, thus reducing Type I errors (ie prohibiting a conduct which is not anti-competitive). Competition authorities and courts could focus their assessment on the economic impact of an allegedly anti-competitive conduct, and apply competition legislation to genuinely anti-competitive unilateral conduct, without having to first analyse whether a dominant position exists.

The Economic Advisory Group argued that the economic approach towards Article 82 implies that there is no need to establish a preliminary and separate assessment of dominance. The emphasis should be on establishing significant competitive harm which is already proof of dominance. Although the Economic Advisory Group specifically refers to proof of dominance, we can apply its argument to firms not being dominant but being able to harm a significant number of consumers. Such conduct should be caught under Article 82 since in the type of market analysed above, the non-dominant firm can induce consumer harm.

We should draw attention to an argument made by the Economic Advisory Group:[48]

> [I]n proposing to reduce the role of separate assessments of dominance and to integrate the substantive assessment of dominance with the procedure for establishing competitive harm itself, we depart from the tradition of case law concerning Art. 82 of the Treaty, but not, we believe,

[47] OECD brief, 'Substantial Market Power' http://www.oecd.org/dataoecd/58/28/41257462.pdf. September 2008.

[48] § 14.

> from the legal norm itself. Article 82 of the Treaty is concerned not just with dominance as such, but with abuses of dominance. *The case law tradition of having separate assessments of dominance and of abusiveness of behaviour simplifies procedures, but this simplification involves a loss of precision in the implementation of the legal norm.*
>
> The structural indicators which traditionally serve as proxies for 'dominance' provide an appropriate measure of power in some markets, but not in others. In a market *where these indicators do not properly measure the firm's ability to impose abusive behaviour on others, the competition authority's intervention under traditional modes of procedure is likely to be inappropriate, too harsh in some cases and too lenient in others.* Given that the Treaty itself does not provide a separate definition of dominance, let alone call for any of the traditionally used indicators as such, it seems more appropriate to have the implementation of the Treaty itself focus on the abuses and to treat the assessment of dominance in this context.[49]

They also argue that:[50]

> This approach also allows us to capture in a balanced and meaningful way the notion of special responsibility of a dominant firm... Since in this analysis we do not need to assess the existence of dominance separately, the special responsibility implicitly applies to any conduct and firm that (is able to) interfere and distort the competitive process of entry into the market.[51]

Both these arguments illustrate a generalization of the application of Article 82 to *any conduct and firm that (is able to) interfere and distort the competitive process of entry into the market.* Such will be the cases of non-dominant firms in a differentiated market, which will not be constrained by the presence of other firms in the market.

The Commission has received criticism for focusing on market shares for a finding of alleged anti-competitive conduct. Such a structural approach towards the definition of dominance protects competitors rather than competition. Such an approach induces harm to consumers. According to Dethmers and Dodoo (2006) the Commission should not focus merely on

[49] Emphasis is by the author.

[50] § 15. Underlining is by the author.

[51] Thus, more than one firm can have this special responsibility since more than one non-dominant firm may have the ability to *interfere and distort the competitive process of entry into the market.*

market shares—an individual assessment should be performed in every decision.[52]

The ability of a firm or firms to restrict output/increase prices, derives from the firm's independent actions. This independence gives the firm market power. However, a firm may enjoy considerable market power, even if it cannot behave to a significant extent independently of its competitors, customers and ultimately consumers.[53] As mentioned above, one of the criticisms of the definition of dominance is that firms cannot act to an appreciable extent independently of their consumers, due to the downward-sloping demand curve which implies that the higher the price of the product the lower the quantity demanded. This inverse relationship between price and quantity may not hold for products such as medicines that are price inelastic, meaning that the increase in price may not affect the quantity demanded. Thus, non-dominant firms which can act independently can be inducing harm to consumers.

In addition, the markets which the Economic Advisory Group refers to in arguing that *the structural indicators which traditionally serve as proxies for 'dominance' provide an appropriate measure of power in some markets, but not in others*, are the type of markets analysed in the example above. In such markets (eg differentiated) focusing on structural indicators (eg market shares) may not be appropriate and *the competition authority's intervention under traditional modes of procedure is likely to be inappropriate, too harsh in some cases and too lenient in others.*

Therefore, Bishop and Walker (2002) argue that the focus on the analysis ought to be on a firm's ability to engage in business activities that prevent effective competition from being maintained.[54] Non-dominant firms can have the ability to adopt conduct that prevents effective competition, and the conduct of such firms should be the focus of the analysis under competition rules.

Häckner (1999)[55] argues that firms in markets with a moderate degree of horizontal differentiation and a moderate degree of concentration are likely to be assessed as having small degree of market dominance. Hence, he notes the correlation between actual market power and assessed market dominance is likely to be weak.

[52] F Dethmers and N Dodoo, 'The Abuse of Hoffman-La Roche: The Meaning of dominance under EC Competition Law' [2006] 27 (10) ECLR 537–549.

[53] R O'Donoghue andJ Padilla, *The Law and Economics of Article 82 EC* (1st edn, Hart Publishing, 2006) 107.

[54] S Bishop and M Walker, *The Economics of EC Competition Law: Concepts, Application and Measurement* (2nd edn, Sweet & Maxwell, 2002) 183.

[55] J Häckner, 'Market Delineation and Product Differentiation' (1999) http://www.ne.su.se/paper/wp99_07.pdf.

In this book we are focusing on the lenient intervention, where the Commission by not being able to apply Article 82 to the anti-competitive conduct of the non-dominant firm in the market, will not safeguard consumer welfare, which is the objective of Article 82. Thus, the Commission will not ensure that this firm bears its responsibility not to *interfere and distort the competitive process of entry into the market.*

The Commission has stated that:

> [A]n undertaking that is capable of substantially increasing prices above the competitive level for a significant period of time holds substantial market power and possesses the requisite ability to act to an appreciable extent independently of competitors, customers and consumers.[56]

It has further added that:

> [T]he fact that an undertaking is compelled by the pressure of its competitors' price reductions to lower its own prices is in general incompatible with the independent conduct which is the hallmark of a dominant position.[57]

In these passages the Commission uses the 'substantial market power' concept to indicate when an undertaking is dominant. As illustrated above, in a differentiated products market more than one firm can have the ability to *increase prices above the competitive level for a significant period of time.* Thus, more than one firm can induce consumer harm, by adopting anti-competitive conduct. Notwithstanding the use of the term *substantial market power* in the Discussion Paper, and the fact that this term can encompass more than one firm in differentiated product markets, the case law has illustrated the apparent inability of the Commission to apply Article 82 to the anti-competitive conduct of non-dominant firms in a differentiated products market.

The gap in the application of Article 82 relates both to exploitative and exclusionary abuses by non-dominant firms. Although the concept of abuse of superior bargaining position/abuse of economic dependence addresses anti-competitive conduct towards other firms, it does not seem to have addressed to date anti-competitive conduct towards consumers. As the above analysis illustrated, the wording of the concept of abuse of economic dependence in some of the jurisdictions implies that in principle such concepts can capture exploitative abuses, but the vast majority of the case law in these countries relates to exclusionary conduct. In some other jurisdictions, the scope of the concept of abuse of economic dependence is even

[56] Discussion Paper Report, § 24.

[57] Discussion Paper Report, § 27.

narrower and applies only to particular sectors or to either the buyer or the supplier side of the market. Thus, Member States that adopt a narrower application of the concept of abuse of superior bargaining position/abuse of economic dependence may not be able to address conduct by non-dominant firms in situations that fall outside the narrow support of these two concepts. It would also be interesting to assess how the abuse of superior bargaining position/abuse of economic dependence concept will be applied in cases concerning the anti-competitive conduct of firms against consumers.

The Commission is unable to address this gap in the application of Article 82, unlike some EU Member States that can apply concepts similar to the one of *abuse of economic dependence* in order to deal with anti-competitive conduct of non-dominant firms. The Commission, although in principle it uses the market share as an indication of dominance, and not the decisive one, has never until now ever condemned a non-dominant firm, for adopting an anti-competitive conduct in a differentiated products market. Had Article 82 been applicable to conduct of non-dominant firms, the Member States would have no need for separate legislation for addressing such conduct, which legislation, we should emphasize, the Commission has respected in Regulation 1/2003, by allowing these Member States to apply such rules.

For example, had the Commission dealt with the *Rossignol*[58] case analysed above, it would not have been able to penalize the undertaking for inducing consumer harm. The small or medium-sized undertaking in question had to be supplied with the products of one particular supplier (Rossignol skis) because they could not be replaced by the products of other suppliers. In the light of Rossignol's market share of about 8 per cent, the *Bundesgerichtshof* denied—for lack of a market-dominating position—that Rossignol had a supply obligation according to section 20 paragraph 1 GWB. *Rossignol* could not be accused under the EC law of having abused the economic dependence of their distributors,[59] and thus the anti-competitive conduct would not have been addressed. In that case, it would have allowed conduct which harms consumers and could be caught under legislation similar to the one in the abovementioned Member States, but not under Article 82.

An indication of the extent of the possible gap in the application of Article 82 is indicated by the fact that in five years, under the legislation on abuse of economic dependence, the Bundeskartellamt initiated more than 100 proceedings, for abuse of purchasing power by major distributors.[60]

[58] KZR 1/75, Rossignol, November 20, 1975, WuW/E BGH, 1391.

[59] C P Correia, P Pinheiro, 'Portugal: Exploitation of Economic Dependence' [2001] 22(8) ECLR N117–119.

[60] See further: I Roudard (1989) 'The New French Legislation on Competition' [1989] 10(2) ECLR 205–232.

A Commission's case which can be identified as a 'gap' case[61] is Bayer (Adalat).[62] Owing to wide price differentials for the product between Spain and France on the one hand and the United Kingdom on the other, there was a surge in parallel trade. In response, Bayer began to restrict supplies to its Spanish and French distributors with the goal of allowing them sufficient stock only for their national markets. Although distributors were still entitled to export the stock which they received, the reduced supplies taken together with the distributors' obligations to supply the national market reduced the scope for parallel exports.

This case concerned Adalat, a product belonging to a category of medicinal products known as calcium antagonists, suitable for treating certain cardiovascular diseases (coronary heart disease, arterial hypertension and congestive heart failure). The scope of the decision was limited to two products in the Adalat range, namely the 10 mg capsule (marketed in the United Kingdom and Spain under the name Adalat and in France under the name Adalate) and the 20 mg modified-release tablet (marketed in the United Kingdom and Spain under the name Adalat-Retard and in France under the name Adalate 20 mg LP).

As regards the geographical market, the Commission held that the relevant markets in this case were the national markets, taking account of the fact that the business of the pharmaceutical industry took place in an essentially national context, marketing authorization for a medicinal product falling exclusively within the competence of the Member States. Moreover, the sale of medicines was influenced by the administrative, and particularly the purchase policies adopted in Member States, especially in France and Spain, where prices were directly set by the competent national authority. Finally, the Commission argued that differences in price-fixing methods and refund arrangements meant that there were wide disparities in the prices of medicinal products in Member States.

As regards the product market, the Commission argued that it is defined by reference to the criterion of identical therapeutic uses for the various competing products. The relevant market was defined as follows:

- Primarily, as far as coronary heart disease and hypertension were concerned, the United Kingdom was deemed to be the major relevant

[61] The Commission does not publish detailed decisions where it states that an abuse has not been substantiated. Although following Regulation 1/2003, the Commission can publish such decisions.

[62] Commission Decision 96/478 *Adalat* [1996] OJ L201/1 (January 10, 1996); Case T-41/96 R *Bayer AG v Commission* [1996] ECR II-381 (Order of June 3, 1996), [2000] ECR II-3383 (Judgment of October 26, 2000); Joined Cases C-2/01 P and C-3/01 P *Bundesverband der Arzneimittel-Importeure eV and Commission v Bayer AG* (Advocate General Opinion of May 22, 2003, ECJ Judgment of January 6, 2004).

market since the agreements directly affected this market by protecting it from parallel imports. The United Kingdom market was the market on which Bayer achieved the largest turnover, through its United Kingdom subsidiary, and on which the effects of the agreements were most clearly identifiable. On this market there had been an observable increase in sales to British customers at British prices.

- Secondarily, as far as coronary heart disease and hypertension were concerned, the markets from which the parallel imports originate, France and Spain, were deemed to be relevant markets since they were artificially closed through the hindrance of parallel exports. On these two markets, the effects of the conduct were clearly evident to the trading partners of Bayer Spain and Bayer France. The wholesalers had seen their export turnover fall very sharply and their business restricted to the domestic market alone.

The market shares held by Bayer with the marketing of Adalat were indicated by reference to the major therapeutic uses of the product. The Commission considered that, in France, Adalat represented a market share of 5.1 per cent on the coronary heart disease market and 4.1 per cent on the hypertension market. In Spain, Adalat represented 7.4 per cent on the coronary heart disease market and 8.7 per cent on the hypertension market. In the United Kingdom, the market shares were 19.6 per cent on the coronary heart disease market and 16.6 per cent on the hypertension market. Finally, in the Community (of 12 Member States), Adalat represented 7.6 per cent of the coronary heart disease market and 5.8 per cent of the hypertension market.

It should be noted that, in the medicinal products sector, doctors and patients are often very attached to a particular brand, particularly in the case of chronic diseases. The Commission argued that this was the case with Adalat, which had the backing of Bayer's name and was recognized as one of the major products worldwide for the treatment of the relevant diseases. It must therefore be borne in mind that, where Adalat was expressly prescribed by the doctor, it was difficult to substitute another, competing product, for example a generic, for it, both for psychological reasons (reluctance on the part of the patient to accept another product) and for statutory reasons (statutory rule in some countries prohibiting pharmacists from substituting a product having equivalent therapeutic properties for the product specifically prescribed by the doctor). The Commission argued that this aspect helped to give the market shares held by Bayer through its product Adalat special significance, these market shares being in themselves already relatively substantial, particularly in the United Kingdom.

The Commission concluded that Bayer's conduct was in breach of Article 81. The Commission held that Bayer had imposed an export ban as part of its continuous commercial relations with the distributors and that this constituted an agreement, particularly given that Bayer had a system in place for detecting exporting wholesalers and that it reduced the amounts supplied to wholesalers who were exporting.

The CFI held that there was no evidence that Bayer had asked its distributors not to export nor that it monitored the final destination of products supplied to them. Instead, the supply thresholds were based on historical supplies, taking into account possible growth in the size of the national market. It added that the Commission was 'wrong in holding that the actual conduct of the wholesalers constitutes sufficient proof in law of their acquiescence in the [manufacturer's] policy designed to prevent parallel imports'. The CFI concluded by taking into account the Commission's argument that an agreement will exist where distributors maintain their commercial relations with a manufacturer which establishes a policy to restrain exports.

The ECJ dismissed the appeals and confirmed that the burden was on the Commission to prove the existence of an agreement. The wholesalers' actions could not be regarded as tacit acquiescence to Bayer's new policy since that policy did not require participation of the wholesalers, nor was acceptance of the policy a precondition for future contractual relations between Bayer and the wholesalers.

The CFI drew a distinction between cases in which an undertaking has adopted a genuinely unilateral measure, and thus without the express or implied participation of another undertaking, and those in which the unilateral character of the measure is merely apparent. The former do not fall within Article 81, they fall within Article 82. It continued by arguing that provided a manufacturer, faced with an event harmful to his interests, adopts a policy without abusing a dominant position, and there is no concurrence of wills between him and his wholesalers, a manufacturer may adopt the supply policy which he considers necessary, even if, by the very nature of its aim, for example, to hinder parallel imports, the implementation of that policy may entail restrictions on competition and affect trade between Member States. Thus, unless the Commission can satisfy the 'rigid' definition of dominance, in the absence of concurrence of wills, an undertaking can adopt measures to protect his interests even if such measures restrict competition.

The ECJ added that the attempt to use Article 81 to penalize an undertaking not in a dominant position which decides to refuse deliveries to wholesalers, in order to prevent them from making parallel exports, disregards the necessary conditions for applying Article 81 and the general system of the Treaty. Under that system, measures adopted by a Member State which prevent parallel exports are indeed prohibited by Article 30 of the Treaty, but unilateral measures taken by private undertakings are subject to restrictions, by virtue of the principles of that Treaty, only if the undertaking in question occupies a dominant position on the market, within the meaning of Article 82, which was not the case in Bayer's conduct.[63]

However, as abovementioned, the Commission had argued that the market shares held by Bayer through its product Adalat had acquired special significance, these market shares being in themselves already relatively substantial, particularly in the United Kingdom. Thus, although Bayer did not have significant market shares in the markets examined by the Commission, the attachment of doctors and patients to particular medicines gave Bayer the ability to adopt conduct which would be harmful for consumers.[64] The Commission and the courts could not apply Article 82, due to the fact that Bayer was not dominant and could not apply Article 81 due to the lack of an agreement between the undertakings emanating from the lack of acquiescence by the other partners, express or implied, to the attitude adopted by the manufacturer.

The result of the *Bayer* case is that an undertaking may adopt a supply policy which it considers necessary even if its nature is to hinder parallel imports, provided that it does so without its abusing dominant position or that there is no concurrence of wills between it and its wholesalers. This implies that an undertaking may adopt a unilateral policy aimed at limiting parallel imports provided it does not constitute a tacit agreement under Article 81 and that its conduct could not be caught under Article 82. If we expand the type of conduct to those in addition to parallel imports, non-dominant undertakings can adopt conduct which induces harm to consumers.

Stothers (2005) in analysing this case argues that this failure to prohibit unilateral action by non-dominant private undertakings to prevent parallel trade appears to be a lacuna in the EC Treaty.[65] Geradin and Petit (2006) note that a 'gap in the EC competition system exists where, as the CFI held in Bayer, a supplier restricts parallel trade without abusing a dominant position, and there is no concurrence of wills between him.'[66] They add that this can, for instance, arise if the supplier is vertically integrated and does not

[63] For the treatment of parallel trading under Article 82 please see further: C-462/06 *Judgment of 22/05/2008, Glaxosmithkline and Laboratoires Glaxosmithkline.*

[64] Parallel imports may have a positive effect on competition by increasing intrabrand competition and lowering prices. It is protected by Arts 28–32 of the EC Treaty as part of the single market principle. Unilateral or multilateral conduct restricting parallel exports or imports is prohibited under those Articles. See further: B McCabe Jedlickova, 'Boundaries Between Unilateral and Multilateral Conducts in Vertical Restraints' [2008] 29 (10) ECLR 600–607.

[65] C Stothers, 'Who Needs Intellectual Property? Competition Law and Restrictions on Parallel Trade within the European Economic Area' [2005] 27 (12) EIPR 458–466.

[66] D Geradin, N Petit, 'Price Discrimination under EC Competition Law: Another Antitrust Doctrine in Search of Limiting Principles?' [2006] 2(3) JCLE 479–531.

enjoy a dominant position on the market. As mentioned above, the CFI in Bayer acknowledged that, in such situation, a manufacturer may adopt the supply policy which he considers necessary, even if the implementation of that policy may entail restrictions on competition.

Hinchliffe (2004) argued that the Commission can try to narrow the definition of the relevant market to cover this kind of anti-competitive restriction of parallel exports to include this unilateral conduct under Article 82.[67] Clearly, such an approach can only lead to Type I errors and legal uncertainty. Barry Hawk notes that 'one of the greatest weaknesses of Community Competition Law'[68] is the treatment by the courts of the boundaries between an agreement, which can be deemed anti-competitive caught by Article 81, and unilateral practices, which can be caught under Article 82, if the undertaking involved is dominant. *Adalat*[69] reduced the possibility of unilaterally imposed policies within continuous business relations coming within the scope of Article 81.

Sousa Ferro (2007)[70] argues that there is a clear trend in the CFI's case law to put an end to unreasonably wide interpretations of the concept of agreement under Article 81,[71] whereas the ECJ has shown itself more reluctant to take this step, the reason being that it is more mindful of the gap which this reform will create in EC competition law. A finding of tacit concurrence in the context of unilaterally imposed policies has been made substantially harder by the *Adalat* case.

The gap that Sousa Ferro (2007) refers to is can be dealt in some jurisdictions with the 'abuse of economic dependency' concept analysed above. A much more effective way to combat such a lacuna in the application of Article 82 in general to unilateral anti-competitive conduct of non-dominant firms is to focus the definition and the application of the concept of dominance on the ability of firms to act independently in their strategies rather than mainly on the market share of the allegedly dominant firms.

We can think of the likelihood of many other similar cases existing where the undertaking had substantial market power in the market and adopted conduct which may have induced harm to consumers. Although following

[67] Hinchliffe (2004) 'When Is an Agreement Not an Agreement?' [2004] 5/6 Business Law Review 108, 110.

[68] B Hawk, 'The American (Anti-Trust) Revolution: Lessons for the EEC?' [1988] ECLR 53, 77.

[69] Commission Decision 96/478 *Adalat* [1996] OJ L201/1 (10 January 1996).

[70] M Sousa Ferro, 'Reassessing Borders between Agreements and Unilateral Practices after Case C-74/04, Volkswagen II' [2007] 28 (3) 205–209.

[71] Sousa Ferro (2007) identified several Commission's decisions which widened the concept of an agreement: *Wea-Filipacchi Music SA* (72/480/CEE), [1972] OJ L303/52; *Miller International Schallplatten GmbH* (76/915/CEE), [1976] OJ L357/40; *The Distillers Company Limited, Conditions of Sale and Price Terms* (78/163/CEE), [1978] OJ L50/16; *Johnson & Johnson* (80/1283/CEE), [1980] OJ L377/16; *Fisher-Price/Quaker Oats Ltd—Toyco* (88/86/CEE), [1988] OJ L49/19; and *Konica* (88/172/CEE), [1988] OJ L78/34.

Regulation 1/2003 the Commission can publish decisions where it states that an abuse has not been substantiated, the Commission does not currently publish such decisions. Thus, even though there is likely to be a significant number of such cases in the case law of the Commission and the courts, identifying such cases is very difficult.

In our analysis we have identified cases dealt at the Member State level, which could not have been addressed by Article 82. As illustrated from the above analysis, the gap in the application of Article 82 is evident, and likely encompasses a large number of cases. The gap includes cases that are addressed at the Member State level by the concept of abuse of economic dependence (applied mainly in exclusionary conduct) and cases that relate to exploitative anti-competitive conduct inducing consumer harm.

The number of cases where non-dominant firms can adopt anti-competitive conduct will mainly depend on the degree of differentiation of the products in the market as well as on the relative market shares of the firms.[72] Due to the limitations created by the requirements for differentiation in the products, for similar market shares and for the adoption of anti-competitive conduct of the non-dominant firm, the number of such cases is likely to be smaller than the number of cases that will deal with abuse of a dominant position. However, the gap in the application of Article 82 does exist and should be addressed in cases dealt with by the Commission as it is addressed in several Member States.

Before we proceed to assess measures that can rectify this gap in the dominance test, it is useful to examine the treatment of anti-competitive conduct of non-dominant firms by the UK as well as the US competition authorities. As the Office of Fair Trading (OFT) guidance on market investigations[73] states, where there is no abuse of a dominant position but structural features of the market nevertheless appear to affect the competitive process adversely, then a market investigation reference will be a possibility. Thus, the UK authorities address the anti-competitive conduct of non-dominant firms by conducting market investigations, rather than by enforcing legislation on the abuse of superior bargaining position/abuse of economic dependence.

According to the response of the UK to the ICN *Questionnaire Abuse of Superior Bargaining Position*,[74] abuse of dominant position law in the UK is geared primarily towards preventing exclusionary conduct, rather than

[72] As mentioned above, the other factors necessary for a finding of an abuse by a non-dominant firm which has market power need to be present (eg high barriers to entry, no objective justification etc).

[73] *Market investigation references*. Guidance about the making of references under Part 4 of the Enterprise Act. www.oft.gov.uk.

[74] http://www.icn-kyoto.org/documents/abuse.html#questionnaire.

protecting undertakings in weaker economic positions from those with superior economic bargaining positions. According to the OFT guidance,[75] market investigations' purpose is to determine whether the process of competition is working effectively in markets as a whole. Market investigations will provide a framework for identifying, analysing and, where appropriate, remedying industry-wide or market-wide competition problems when there is no adequate basis for addressing under the Competition Act 98 (which addresses anti-competitive agreements and unilateral conduct).

The OFT will only make references to the Competition Commission ('CC') when each of the following criteria has been met:[76]

- it would not be more appropriate to deal with the competition issues identified by applying the Competition Act 1998 (CA98) or using other powers available to the OFT or, where appropriate, to sectoral regulators;
- it would not be more appropriate to address the problem identified by means of undertakings in lieu of a reference;
- the scale of the suspected problem, in terms of its adverse effect on competition, is such that a reference would be an appropriate response to it;
- there is a reasonable chance that appropriate remedies will be available.

Thus, the OFT will go on to consider a reference to the CC in one of two circumstances:

- when it has reasonable grounds to suspect that there are market features, which prevent, restrict or distort competition, but not to establish a breach of the CA98 prohibitions;
- when action under CA98 has been or is likely to be ineffective for dealing with the adverse effect on competition identified.

The Enterprise Act 2002 provides for market investigations to be carried out by the Competition Commission of the conduct that prevents, restricts or distorts competition. Following a reference it will be for the CC to decide whether competition is indeed prevented, restricted or distorted and (if so) what, if any, action should be taken to remedy the adverse effect on competition or any detrimental effect on customers resulting from it. The harm may be in the form of higher prices, lower quality or less choice of goods or services, or less innovation in relation to goods or services in any market in the UK.

[75] *Market investigation references*. Guidance about the making of references under Part 4 of the Enterprise Act. www.oft.gov.uk.

[76] See further: section 131 of the Enterprise Act and *Market investigation references*. Guidance about the making of references under Part 4 of the Enterprise Act. www.oft.gov.uk

Section 131(2) of the Act states that, for the purpose of a market investigation reference, a feature of a market in the United Kingdom shall be construed as:

(a) the structure of the market concerned or any aspect of that structure;
(b) any conduct (whether or not in the market concerned) of one or more than one person who, supplies or acquires goods or services in the market concerned; or
(c) any conduct relating to the market concerned of customers of any person who supplies or acquires goods or services.

Conduct includes any failure to act, whether intentional or not and any other unintentional conduct. The CC will have regard to any conduct of the firms in a market (whether sellers or buyers) that could, in the circumstances of the particular market, have an adverse effect on competition (whether in the market in which the firms themselves are engaged or in some other market, for example, the market of the sellers' suppliers or customers). The Competition Commission may require remedial measures as it considers reasonable and practicable to mitigate or prevent the adverse effect on competition or any detrimental effects on customers.[77]

A firm may have market power, and the capacity to act in ways that may prevent, restrict or distort competition, with a market share below that usually regarded as necessary to suggest dominance for the purposes of CA98. For example, the Competition Commission may assess the effects on competition of certain forms of discounts and rebates. In many cases, discounts and rebates are normal components of the competitive process and will, in general, not be a cause for concern. However, where a firm has market power then the CC will consider whether any discounts or rebates offered might have adverse effects on competition. Thus, the CC approach towards discounts and rebates encompasses the assessment of such conduct by firms having market power and which are not necessarily dominant. The Commission cannot address conduct involving discounts or rebates unless the undertaking is dominant, curtailing thus its ability to capture anti-competitive conduct by non-dominant firms.

The ability to adopt anti-competitive conduct will depend upon the effectiveness of the constraints exerted by its competitors or its customers. Where there is no abuse of a dominant position but structural features of the market nevertheless appear to affect the competitive process adversely, then a market investigation reference will be a possibility. Thus, adverse effects on competition induced by conduct that does not involve either

[77] *Market Investigation References: Competition Commission Guidelines*, www.competition-commission.org.uk.

agreements between undertakings or abuses of dominance, although beyond the reach of CA98 this can be addressed by market investigation references. Such conduct is likely to include competition problems arising from uncoordinated parallel conduct by several firms or industry-wide features of a market in cases where the OFT does not have reasonable grounds to suspect the existence of anti-competitive agreements or dominance. Thus, if the market structure is such that non-dominant firms can induce consumer harm, the OFT and the CC can address such conduct by conducting a market investigation and adopting measures that will rectify this harm.

On the other hand the Commission does not have the ability to address such anti-competitive conduct of non-dominant firms, an inability which induces consumer welfare harm and exacerbates Type II errors (ie not capturing anti-competitive conduct of non-dominant firms) in competition enforcement.

After presenting the UK approach in addressing conduct of non-dominant firms, the focus turns on the ability of the US competition authorities to address conduct which does not fall within the ambit of Sherman Act but which induce harm to consumers. The US FTC Act provides the clearest example of legislation that is able to address gaps similar to the gap in the enforcement of Article 82. The Section 5 of the FTC Act enables the Federal Trade Commission (FTC) to capture conduct that cannot be addressed by the Sherman Act.

> **§ 45. Unfair methods of competition unlawful; prevention by Commission**
>
> **(a) Declaration of unlawfulness; power to prohibit unfair practices; inapplicability to foreign trade**
>
> (1) Unfair methods of competition in or affecting commerce, and unfair or deceptive acts or practices in or affecting commerce, are hereby declared unlawful.
>
> (2) The Commission is hereby empowered and directed to prevent persons, partnerships, or corporations, except banks, savings and loan institutions described in section 57a(f)(3) of this title, Federal credit unions described in section 57a(f)(4) of this title, common carriers subject to the Acts to regulate commerce, air carriers and foreign air carriers subject to part A of subtitle VII of title 49, and persons, partnerships, or corporations insofar as they are subject to the Packers and Stockyards Act, 1921, as amended (7 U.S.C. 181 et seq), except as provided in section 406(b) of said Act (7 U.S.C. 227(b)), from using unfair methods of competition in or affecting commerce and unfair or deceptive acts or practices in or affecting commerce.
>
> (3) This subsection shall not apply to unfair methods of competition

involving commerce with foreign nations (other than import commerce) unless—

(A) such methods of competition have a direct, substantial, and reasonably foreseeable effect—

(i) on commerce which is not commerce with foreign nations, or on import commerce with foreign nations; or

(ii) on export commerce with foreign nations, of a person engaged in such commerce in the United States; and

(B) such effect gives rise to a claim under the provisions of this subsection, other than this paragraph. If this subsection applies to such methods of competition only because of the operation of subparagraph (A)(ii), this subsection shall apply to such conduct only for injury to export business in the United States.

Commissioner Leibowitz (2008) mentions that Senator Cummins of Iowa, one of the main proponents of the FTC Act, emphasized that the reason for the law was, 'to go further and make some things offenses' that were not condemned by the antitrust laws. He added that 'the only purpose of Section 5 [is] to make some things punishable, to prevent some things, that cannot be punished or prevented under antitrust law.'[78] And Leibowitz (2008) adds that Congress could have simply given the Commission the ability to enforce the Sherman Act. But it didn't. Instead, the plain text of the statute makes it clear that Congress intended to create an agency with authority that extended well beyond the limits of the antitrust laws.

The US courts in cases such as *Keppel Brothers*,[79] *FTC v Brown Shoe Company*[80] and *FTC v Motion Picture Advertising Service Company*,[81] have affirmed the ability of the FTC to apply the FTC Act.

In *FTC v Sperry & Hutchinson*, Justice White speaking for a unanimous view of the court posed and answered two questions:

> The question [of the reach of Section 5] is a double one: first, does Section 5 empower the Commission to define and proscribe an unfair competitive practice, even though the practice does not infringe either the letter or the spirit of the antitrust laws. Second, does Section 5 empower the Commission to proscribe practices as unfair or deceptive in their effect upon consumers regardless of their nature or quality as competition? We think the statute, its legislative history and prior cases compel an affirmative answer to both questions.

[78] J Leibowitz, 'Tales from the Crypt', FTC Workshop on Section 5, 17 October 2008, www.ftc.gov.

[79] *FTC v RF Keppel & Bros Inc* 291 US 304, 310 (1934).

[80] *FTC v Brown Shoe Co*, 384 US 316, 321 (1966).

[81] *Federal Trade Commission v Motion Picture Advertising Service Co* 344 US 392 (1953).

> Legislative and judicial authorities alike convince us that the Federal Trade Commission does not arrogate excessive power to itself if, in measuring a practice against the elusive, considers public values beyond simply those enshrined in the letter or encompassed in the spirit of the antitrust laws.[82]

The Supreme Court's decision in this case adopts an expansive reading of section 5 of the FTC Act. The Supreme Court held that section 5 enables the FTC to 'define and proscribe an unfair competitive practice, even though the practice does not infringe either the letter or the spirit of the antitrust laws' and to 'proscribe practices as unfair or deceptive in their effect on competition.'[83] In addition the majority Statement for the FTC *In the Matter of Negotiated Data Solutions LLC* states that the Act reaches 'not only practices that violate the Sherman Act and other antitrust laws, but also practices that the Commission determines are against public policy for other reasons.'[84]

Thus, Section 5 of the FTC Act addresses a gap that is left by the inability of Sherman Act to apply to certain anti-competitive conduct. The Commission does not have the ability to capture the equivalent gap in Article 82 at all.

Creighton et al (2008) argue that section 5 applies, inter alia, to 'gap-filling' cases, that is cases that may satisfy the economic requirements of antitrust, but fail one of the legal elements of section 1 (usually the 'agreement' requirement) or section 2 (usually the 'monopoly power' element).[85] The type of gap-filling cases Creighton et al have identified[86] as the ones

[82] *FTC v Sperry & Hutchinson*, 405 US 223, 239, 244 (1972). The court in *FTC v Brown Shoe Co* 384 US 316, 321 (1966) stated that '[t]his broad power of the Commission is particularly well established with regard to trade practices which conflict with the basic policies of the Sherman Act and Clayton Acts even though such practices may not actually violate these laws . . .'; In *FTC v Ind Fed'n of Dentists*, 476 US 447, 454 (1986) the court argued that observing that the standard for 'unfairness' under the FTC Act is, 'by necessity, an elusive one, encompassing not only practices that violate the Sherman Act and the other antitrust laws, but also practices that the Commission determines are against public policy for other reasons'. See further: D Balto, 'A Section 5 Enforcement Agenda That Even Bill O'Reilly Could Love', FTC Workshop on Section 5, 17 October 2008, www.ftc.gov.

[83] At 239.

[84] See Statement of the Commission, *In the Matter of Negotiated Data Solutions LLC*, FTC File No. 051 0094 (23 January 2008), available at http://www.ftc.gov/os/caselist/0510094/080122statement.pdf. Dissenting Statement of Chairman Majoras, *In the Matter of Negotiated Data Solutions LLC*, FTC File No 051 0094 (23 January 2008), available at http://www.ftc.gov/os/caselist/0510094/080122majoras.pdf; Dissenting Statement of Commissioner Kovacic, *In the Matter of Negotiated Data Solutions LLC*, FTC File No 051 0094 (Jan. 23, 2008), available at http://www.ftc.gov/os/caselist/0510094/080122kovacic.pdf. See further: T Leary.

[85] S Creighton et al, 'Some Thoughts About the Scope of Section 5' FTC Workshop on Section 5, 17 October 2008, www.ftc.gov.

[86] Invitations to collude, (FTC's consent order in *Valassis, In the Matter of Valassis*

falling under the jurisdiction of section 5 of the FTC Act, cannot be addressed by the Commission by applying Article 82. Thus, the gap in the applicability of antitrust laws that section 5 rectifies, is not addressed by Article 82. The anti-competitive conduct that escapes the application of Sherman Act are addressed in the US, whereas the anti-competitive conduct that escapes the application of Article 82 (and of the national equivalents) is not addressed at all, resulting in inadequate competition enforcement.

Foyer (2008) claims that strategic unilateral withholding by a non-monopolist would arguably violate section 5, but possibly not the Sherman Act, if there is highly inelastic demand at a time of peak capacity utilization and such withholding undermines efficiency in the market. The market structure in the example that Foyer presents (ie capacity constraints and low elasticity of demand due, inter alia, to differentiation) to illustrate the applicability of section 5 is very similar to the market structure that we have analysed herein, where conduct of non-dominant firms induces harm to consumers and cannot be addressed by Article 82. Thus, the FTC can address anti-competitive conduct of non-dominant firms in such markets but the Commission cannot capture such conduct under Article 82.

Specifically Foyer (2008) adds that 'unilateral withholding may be an example of a non-monopolist dominant firm, perhaps defined with respect to the price sensitivity of the residual demand it faces, abusing its position of power and engaging in an unfair method of competition, and that both the FTC and the EU could likely agree on a statement to this effect.'[87] The FTC by employing section 5 would be able to address such a conduct. It is highly questionable whether the Commission would be in a position to address such a conduct by a non-dominant firm under Article 82.

Balto (2008) identified several industries where section 5 could be clearly enforceable. He argues that there are a wide variety of practices that insurance companies engage which undermine and threaten to undermine the competitive process and ultimately harm consumers. As regards the health-

Communications, Inc., No 51-0008 (14 March 2006), available at http://www.ftc.gov/os/caselist/0510008/060314cmp0510008.pdf). Creighton et al add that the FTC's *Ethyl* case might have been a gap filling cases. Finally, they add that patent fishing (firms acquire patents and then demand payments from probable non-infringers, but where the payments are much less than the costs of litigation) also constitutes a gap filling case. The authors argue that section 5 may also apply to, what they call, 'frontier' cases where all of the legal requirements for a Sherman Act claim are met, but the claim involves new forms of anti-competitive conduct that fall outside traditional categories of antitrust analysis. Former FTC Commissioner Thomas Leary has made strong arguments for the application of section 5 in this context. In addition, 'yes, but' cases are ones that meet all the economic and legal requirements of a Sherman Act claim, but cannot be brought under the Sherman Act because of legal limitations imposed for reasons unrelated to antitrust. See further: S Creighton et al, 'Some Thoughts *About the Scope of Section 5*' FTC Workshop on Section 5, 17 October 2008, www.ftc.gov, 2.

[87] A Foyer, 'Section 5 as Bridge Towards Convergence', FTC Workshop on Section 5, 17 October 2008, www.ftc.gov, 7.

care intermediary markets, he argued that several intermediary markets are very concentrated and have significant barriers to entry. Intermediaries can use their power to foreclose competition through a wide variety of exclusionary practices. He added that where the practices of the intermediaries are not wholly transparent, there may be opportunities for deceptive conduct. A related market where Balto thinks section 5 should apply to the pharmacy benefit managers market as they adopt several types of conduct which can harm consumer welfare. Finally, he adds that although the original purpose of group purchasing organizations was to obtain better pricing on products than hospitals could obtain individually, and to provide value-added services, and such organizations may reduce purchase costs by giving hospitals greater bargaining power, the growing consolidation in the market and the resulting market power has increased the exclusionary potential of some of group purchasing organizations. Balto's examples are focused on US markets, but we can draw several parallels with markets across the EU. Such conduct of non-dominant firms cannot be addressed by Article 82.

Balto (2008) adds that to the extent that potential enforcement actions against market share discounts, or other forms of de facto exclusivity seem deficient for some element necessary for a Sherman Act challenge, section 5 may enable the FTC to overcome that deficiency.

We should emphasize Balto's argument that the Congress that enacted the FTC Act created section 5 to enable the FTC to utilize its expertise to challenge practices that were not technical antitrust violations. He adds that the FTC should begin to use those powers in a careful and prudent fashion, bringing enforcement actions that will bring significant benefits to consumers. The Commission unfortunately has no such ability neither to address any of the above-mentioned kinds of anti-competitive conduct, nor to address any conduct that may be adopted by a non-dominant firm and induce harm to consumers.

Salinger (2008),[88] argues that section 5 can fill in gaps left by the other statutes. As examples of such gaps he mentions invitations to collude, as well as facilitating practices. He adds that because section 2 outlaws only monopolization, another possible gap in the Sherman Act is anti-competitive behavior that creates market power short of monopoly. This is very similar to the gap in Article 82 due to its inability to apply to anti-competitive conduct of non-dominant firms. He adds that when the FTC uses section 5 alone, it should do so to attack anti-competitive behavior that falls into gaps left by the Sherman and Clayton Acts. The Commission has no such 'tool' to address the enforcement gaps left by the inability of applying Article 82 to the anti-competitive conduct of non-dominant firms.

[88] Remarks of Michael Salinger at the FTC Workshop on Section 5, 17 October 2008, www.ftc.gov.

The argument made herein as regards the need for Article 82 to apply to non-dominant firms is echoed in the comments of Albert Foyer, president of the American Antitrust Institute.[89] In the context of the Sherman Act, Foyer argues that a firm which is dominant in practice and which engages in an unfair method of competition should be subject to section 5 even if its market share is less than the 70 per cent that often characterizes Sherman Act decisions.[90] He adds that section 5 can and should be applied with a realistic and practical assessment of a firm's ability and incentives to exercise market power and its effects. We echo this argument and emphasize the need for the ability of Article 82 to address anti-competitive conduct by firms which have the ability and incentives to exploit their market power.

In providing some examples of violations of section 5 which are not considered to be violations of Sherman Act, he mentions unilateral withholding and argues that a successful withholding strategy 'appears to require highly inelastic demand on the part of consumers and a temporary situation that can be exploited by a strategically situated, but not necessarily monopolistic, firm.'[91]

In this chapter we have addressed the gap in the application of Article 82, which is principally based on the differentiation of products leading to low elasticity for the demand of the product. Due to the fact that the differentiation of products induces customer inertia, customers are likely to continue buying them even if their price increases. As mentioned above, customer inertia bestows market power to the non-dominant undertaking and allows it to adopt anti-competitive conduct.

[89] A Foyer, 'Section 5 as Bridge Towards Convergence', FTC Workshop on Section 5, 17 October 2008, www.ftc.gov.

[90] The US Supreme Court has indicated that market shares above 66 per cent indicate monopoly power without clearly specifying the lower boundary. See *US v DuPont* (1956) 351 US 377, 379.

[91] A Foyer, 'Section 5 as Bridge Towards Convergence', FTC Workshop on Section 45, 17 October 2008, www.ftc.gov, 5.

CHAPTER 5

How to Rectify the Gap

Germany in its response to the questionnaire of the ICN on abuse of superior bargaining position argued that '[t]he German legislator, when incorporating the section 20 (2) ARC into antitrust law in 1973, held the view that not only conduct by those undertakings holding a dominant position could distort competition. In fact, the conduct of undertakings, which were able to exercise market power only to a certain extent and in relation to certain undertakings was also deemed to be capable of having negative effects on competition.'[1]

We should note, as abovementioned, that the origins of the notion of dominance can be traced back to German competition law. The German competition law (*Gesetz gegen Wettbewerbsbeschränkungen* (GWB)[2]) used the term 'dominance' in section 22(1); it was a familiar concept due to the previous Abuse Regulation of 1923.[3] Thus, 50 years after the inclusion of the concept of dominance in the legislation, the German legislator identified the lack in the enforcement ability and decided to address the concept of abuse of economic dependence/abuse of superior bargaining position.

Italy argued that underpinning the abuse of economic dependence provisions is that in long-term contractual relations characterized by a significant imbalance in the bargaining position of the parties, some firms may indeed be in the same position as end consumers vis-à-vis their contractual counterpart and should therefore be granted some protection against the risk of exploitation.'[4]

Japan argued that its willingness to address the ASBP stems from the idea that ASBP undermines 'the foundation of the free competition' in cases where a party in a superior bargaining position, by making use of that position, restrains the independent business activities of the other party and forces the other party to accept disadvantages that it would not if the competition worked properly.

[1] 'ICN Special Program for Kyoto Annual Conference Report on Abuse of Superior Bargaining Position', www.internationalcompetitionnetwork.org. ('ICN Kyoto-ASBP') 15.

[2] Available from the Bundeskartellamt website http://www.bundeskartellamt.de/wDeutsch/index.shtml?navid=27.

[3] Verordnung Gegen Missbrauch Wirtschaftlicher Machtstellungen, 1923, Reichsbesetzblatt, [R6B.1] I, 1067, 2 November 1923.

[4] 'ICN Special Program for Kyoto Annual Conference Report on Abuse of Superior Bargaining Position', www.internationalcompetitionnetwork.org 15.

Thus, the rationale of countries that have legislation addressing concepts such as abuse of superior bargaining position/abuse of economic dependence is the inability of Article 82 type legislation to capture all anti-competitive conduct.

As regards the gap in the application of Article 82, the concept of dominance is found in two sets of legal provisions, namely Article 82[5] and the ECMR.[6] The original ECMR[7] did not expressly refer to the notion of a dominant position on the part of one or more undertakings. Article 2(3) of the original ECMR states that: 'A concentration which creates or strengthens a dominant position as a result of which effective competition would be significantly impeded in the common market or in a substantial part of it shall be declared incompatible with the common market'. By focusing on 'the creation or strengthening of a dominant position', it employed a language reminiscent of that used in Article 82.

The Recast ECMR[8] is applied ex ante, and thus the focus is on the changes in the structure of the market that come as a consequence of the merger. The purpose of the merger control is not to prevent future abuses of a dominant position, but to ensure that the post-merger market structure will not be less competitive.

Article 82 is applied ex post and thus the focus is on the past conduct of the undertaking and on the operation of the market during that period. In addition, Article 82 focuses on market behaviour,[9] while the focus of both the original and the Recast ECMR is on the future market structure rather than on the past development of competition in the market. The Commission changed the substantive test for mergers from the dominance test[10] to the Significant Impediment to Effective Competition test ('SIEC')[11] in order to capture mergers in differentiated product markets that could have escaped merger control.[12] Thus, the Commission realized the gap in the dominance test and rectified it.

[5] Articles 81 and 82 of the EC Treaty (ex 85 and 86 prior to the Treaty of Amsterdam which came into force on 1 May 1999. Article 12 of the Treaty of Amsterdam provided for the renumbering of the EC Treaty Articles). The EC Treaty was signed on 25 March 1957.

[6] Article 82 deals with the abuse of an already existing dominant position (ex post), whereas the ECMR deals with the prospective assessment of dominance (ex ante).

[7] Council Regulation (EEC) 4064/89 of 21 December 1989 on the control of concentrations between undertakings [1989] OJ L395/1, corrigendum [1990] OJ L257/14.

[8] Council Regulation (EC) No 139/2004 of 20 January 2004 on the control of concentrations between undertakings (the EC Merger Regulation), (Recast ECMR), OJ L 24, 1–22.

[9] See further: P Roth, *Bellamy and Child European Community Law of Competition* (5th edn, Sweet and Maxwell, London, 2001) 405.

[10] Council Regulation (EEC) 4064/89 of 21 December 1989 on the control of concentrations between undertakings [1989] OJ L395/1, corrigendum [1990] OJ L257/14.

[11] Regulation 139/2004.

[12] These cases are referred as gap cases. The 'gap' in the dominance test corresponds to the situation where the post-merger entity's market power would not amount to single firm or collective dominance but where the merger may nonetheless lead to non-coordinated effects in

As Faull and Nikpay (2007) argue, there is no reason to believe that the concept of dominance in the original ECMR[13] has a different meaning from the concept of dominance in Article 82.[14] The introduction of the concept of dominance in merger control pointed in the direction of the ECJ in Article 82 cases, even though jurisprudence focuses on abusive commercial conduct by dominant firms rather than on the preservation of competitive market structures.[15]

Since the Commission recognized the gap in the dominance test in the original ECMR and changed the substantive test, in order to capture the merger gap cases, why does the Commission not address the same gap in the dominance test in Article 82 cases?

As the abovementioned analysis indicates, the concept of dominance has the same meaning under merger control and Article 82. The same market structure that can lead to a gap merger case (eg differentiated products market, few strong firms in the post-merger market, limited switching, capacity constraints etc) can lead to a gap case in Article 82 as was illustrated above. The Commission seems, under the new merger substantive test, to prevent the creation of a firm that can lead to non-coordinated effects in the post merger oligopolistic market (ie gap case) but cannot prevent this firm from adopting anti-competitive conduct in the post-merger market.

This is counterintuitive since the dominance test under the original ECMR was 'devised' from the dominance concept under Article 82. In fact,

oligopolistic markets. The gap refers to situations where the remaining firms in the post-merger market have the incentive and ability to adopt conduct inducing an adverse impact on competition, and thus profit from exerting their market power in the post-merger market, without being dependent upon a coordinated response on the part of the other members of the oligopolistic market structure. The adverse impact on competition is induced by the merger.

Gap cases arise in oligopolistic markets which exhibit factors conducive to collective dominance (coordinated effects). Such factors include: barriers to entry and exit, a small number of firms, ability to coordinate towards equilibrium, ability to enforce compliance as well as ability to monitor and deter any prospective maverick firms. These criteria depend on features such as product homogeneity, low demand growth, low price sensitivity of demand, symmetric cost structures and multi market contacts (I Kokkoris, 'The Development of the Concept of Collective Dominance in the European Community Merger Regulation from its Inception to its Current Status' World Competition, September 2007). In particular in differentiated product markets where a merger can lead to incentives for conduct having an adverse impact on competition, without creating a single leading player, and without significantly increasing the feasibility of tacit collusion. The latter situation, which cannot be dealt either as single-firm dominance or as collective dominance, is known as the 'gap' in the application of the dominance test.

[13] Council Regulation (EEC) 4064/89 of 21 December 1989 on the control of concentrations between undertakings, [1989] OJ L395/1, corrigendum [1990] OJ L257/14.

[14] J Faull and A Nikpay, *The EC Law of Competition* (Oxford University Press, UK, 2007) 322.

[15] See further: C J Cook and C S Kerse, *EC Merger Control* (3rd edn, Sweet and Maxwell, London, 2000) 131.

prior to the adoption of the original ECMR, the Commission used Article 82 to address the anti-competitive effects arising from a merger. In *Re Continental Can*[16] the Commission found an abuse of Article 82 where a takeover bid was made by a dominant undertaking for a smaller competitor. The Commission argued that such an acquisition might constitute an abuse since it would adversely affect the structure of competition in a market where competition was weakened from the presence of the allegedly dominant undertaking. The ECJ annulled the Commission's decision on the basis that it did not identify the market accurately. However, the ECJ confirmed that Article 82 could apply in a situation where a dominant undertaking was acquiring another undertaking.[17]

Thus, if the dominance test in merger control cannot capture some mergers in certain types of market structure, it cannot capture unilateral conduct under Article 82 in the same types of market structure. Since the Commission addressed the gap in the original ECMR why has the Commission not addressed the same gap in Article 82?

As abovementioned, the Economic Advisory Group for Competition Policy argued that the effects-based approach needs to put less weight on a separate verification of dominance and focus on sustaining a consistent and verifiable assessment of significant competitive harm.

> In proposing to reduce the role of separate assessments of dominance and to integrate the substantive assessment of dominance with the procedure for establishing competitive harm itself, we depart from the tradition of case law concerning Art 82 of the Treaty, but not, we believe, from the legal norm itself. The case law tradition of having separate assessments of dominance and of abusiveness of behaviour simplifies procedures, but this simplification involves a loss of precision in the implementation of the legal norm.[18]

A means to rectify the gap in the application of Article 82 would be to place less importance on proving whether a firm is dominant by placing unwarranted focus on the market share of the firm and focus on whether the firm has the market power to adopt anti-competitive conduct in the market. In a differentiated products market more than one firm has the ability to adopt such conduct, and following the wording of the case law, in the definition

[16] *Europemballage Corporation* [1972] OJ L7/14.

[17] As far as Article 82 is concerned, its shortcomings as regards to its application in merger assessment relate to the fact that it applies to concentrations already enjoying a dominant position. A transaction which creates a dominant position, as may be the case with a merger or acquisition falls outside the ambit of Article 82.

[18] EAGCP Report.

of the concept of dominance,[19] more than one firm may be able to behave *independently of its competitors, its customers and ultimately of consumers*.

The definition of dominance refers to the ability of the firm to behave independently from the competitive constraints that the allegedly dominant firm faces. This definition does not necessarily imply that there can only be one dominant firm in the market. This is likely to be the case in most homogenous markets. In differentiated markets more than one firm can act *independently of its competitors, its customers and ultimately of consumers*, and thus in principle, more than one firm can be deemed to be dominant.

According to the Commission, the market share is only an indication of dominance and is employed as an initial filter. Following this approach the Commission has found companies with high market shares as not being dominant and firms with low market shares as being dominant. What it has not been able to allege is that the non-dominant firm induces consumer harm and thus should be penalized. By attaching so much importance on the actual market shares compared to the relative market shares, the Commission has never found the second biggest firm in the market to abuse its power. By adopting a more flexible approach towards the relative market share levels of the incumbents in a market, the Commission should be able to amend this inability and thus argue that the second biggest firm is dominant/possesses substantial market power, and thus adopting anti-competitive conducts which are harmful for consumers in the market. The Commission has the chance to clarify its position and rectify the gap in the next step of the Discussion Paper. The Commission in the Guidance Paper argues that there may be specific cases below that threshold where competitors are not in a position to constrain effectively the conduct of a dominant undertaking, for example where they face serious capacity limitations. In such cases the Commission may also investigate anticompetitive conducts. Although the Commission makes an attempt to apply Article 82 on firms having low market shares which are able though to adopt anticompetitive conducts, it does not liberate the analysis from the factor of dominance. Thus, non-dominant firms having low market shares in differentiated product markets or in markets where capacity constraints are significant, can still adopt anticompetitive conducts and harm consumer welfare.[20]

The Commission may instead wish to issue a Notice on the treatment of abuse of superior bargaining position/abuse of economic dependence.

[19] Case 27/76, *United Brands Co and United Brands Continental BV v Commission* [1978], ECR I-207.

[20] Changing the wording of Article 82 in the EC Treaty is the most complicated means of rectifying the gap in the application of Article 82. At present (September 2008) the EC is likely to issue administrative priority guidelines for Article 82 cases.

Certain issues that may arise in pursuing this option is that not all Member States have such legislation. Thus, it may be difficult for all Member States to agree on this new soft legislation. However, we should note that not all Member States have leniency provisions in their legislation or the SIEC test as their substantive test for merger assessment,[21] but agreed to a leniency notice and to a new merger regulation based on the SIEC test.

As regards addressing the conduct of non-dominant firms due to some difficulties in changing the EC Treaty in order to include such provision in the legislation rectifying the gap through the future case law development may prove to be a more desirable means of addressing the inability of Article 82 and of some relevant national provisions to apply to non-dominant firms inducing consumer harm.

The Commission as well as the national authorities should avoid a structural approach to the definition of dominance but rather look at the ability of the undertaking to behave *independently of its competitors, its customers and ultimately of consumers*.[22] They should look at the market in a dynamic analytical frame in assessing whether the conduct of non-dominant firms (eg the second largest firm) in the market harms consumer welfare and thus should be sanctioned. Such development in the Commission's decisional practice bears the risk of appeal to the CFI/ECJ.

It is my belief that such risk is acceptable and should be taken by the Commission and other competition authorities in order to advance the enforcement of competition legislation and to improve competition policy. Although there may be some successful appeals against the initial decisional practice of the authorities, the authorities as well as the courts will need to 'adapt' to a less structural approach to the dominance concept which will ensure that all anti-competitive conduct of non-dominant firms inducing consumer harm can be addressed.

An argument against the ability of the Commission to capture harmful conduct of non-dominant firms relates to the possible localized nature of such conduct (especially that related to abuse of superior bargaining position/abuse of economic dependence). Some of the cases presented herein illustrate that such conduct may not be de minimis. Even though the latter conduct may be de minimis in some cases, the Commission as well as some Member States (which do not have such legislation) will be able to address conduct of non-dominant firms which may be harming consumer welfare and of course will not be de minimis.[23]

[21] Notably large Member States such as Italy and Germany which fiercely opposed the change in the substantive legal test for merger assessment.

[22] Case 27/76, *United Brands Co. and United Brands Continental BV v Commission* [1978] ECR I-207.

[23] An interesting question arises as to whether the Commission should be able to address harmful conduct which cannot be caught by the abuse of dominance legislation of Member States.

An argument can be made that the Commission by rectifying this gap, will have much wider discretion in the investigations that it initiates and that may cause firms to be less resilient in their product development. We should echo Leary's (ex-FTC Commissioner) argument[24] in relation to section 5 of the FTC Act, which as abovementioned addresses the anti-competitive conduct that cannot be addressed by the Sherman Act.[25] Leary (2008) notes that section 5 should not be employed simply as '*an easier path that might lead to more short-term victories*'.

In this respect we should also emphasize Commissioner's Leibowitz arguments as regards the applicability of section 5. He argues that the FTC's 'powers to restrict unfair methods of competition, consistent with Congressional intent, should only extend to those anti-competitive schemes or practices that harm consumers. It should not be enough for the Commission to show just that a firm acted inconsistently with normally acceptable business behavior, because Congress did not create the Commission to be a national nanny or to mediate between firms that can generally protect themselves where consumers are not at risk. At the same time, however, the Commission should not be tied to the more technical definitions of consumer harm that limit applications of the Sherman Act when we are looking at pure Section 5 violations.'[26]

Apparently, and correctly, the FTC is curtailing its discretion of applying Section 5 of the FTC Act and applies it *to those anti-competitive schemes or practices that harm consumers*. The Commission is likely to adopt a similar discretion and will not 'disproportionately' apply Article 82 to the conduct of non-dominant undertakings. The Commission has already 'proved' the 'careful' approach towards the applicability of the new ECMR on anti-competitive mergers. Although concerns on the Commission's wider discretion had been raised prior to its adoption, the Commission four years after the new ECMR has not 'disproportionately' applied the new ECMR. Rather the new ECMR (and the new test which does not depend on dominance) has significantly improved the Commission's accuracy and efficiency in merger assessment.

Importantly the concern of expansive discretion of the Commission relates to a possible mitigation in the innovation in which firms would be involved in, for fear of being found to have adopted an anti-competitive conduct. Higher innovation by firms may lead to higher quality products and thus enhance consumer welfare. Whether the anti-competitive conduct, eg price

24 T Leary, 'The Search for Consensus on the Revival of Section 5', FTC Workshop on Section 5, 17 October 2008, www.ftc.gov.

25 Thus, section 5 addresses a gap identical to the gap in the application of Article 82 that cannot be addressed by the Commission.

26 J Leibowitz, 'Tales from the Crypt', FTC Workshop on Section 5, 17 October 2008, www.ftc.gov.

discrimination, that a non-dominant firm may be involved in, will lead to the firm rationalizing its revenues and thus being able to invest in higher innovation and improved product line, will depend on how competitive the market for the firm's products is and more generally on the incentives that the non-dominant firm may have to pass on the accrued monetary benefits to the consumers in the form of improved product line.

In a differentiated product market, where the non-dominant firm possesses market power, its incentives to pass on any benefits obtained from the anti-competitive conduct to its customers are questionable. In addition, in case the anti-competitive conduct leads to efficiencies which benefit consumers the non-dominant firm can attempt to objectively justify the conduct.

The same concern as regards the decrease in the innovation and of research and development ('R&D') of firms was raised in the debate prior to the adoption of the new ECMR. However, these fears did not materialize. There is no particular reason to expect that such fears of 'over enforcement' leading to a hampering of innovation and of R&D in general will materialize if the Commission rectifies the gap in Article 82. In addition, innovation is essential in industries with high R&D. Thus, in the majority of industries any mitigation in innovation is not likely to lead to consumer harm more significant than the one induced by allowing the non-dominant firms to adopt anti-competitive conduct.

In addressing the anti-competitive conduct of non-dominant firms, the Commission is likely to make Type I errors and lead to creating concern amongst firms as regards the conduct that they can adopt in order to compete in the market. It is better to address conduct of non-dominant firms and risk some Type I errors (ie prohibiting a conduct which is not anti-competitive), possibly inducing a chilling effect in the innovation activities of firms, rather than accept the possible Type II errors (not capturing anti-competitive conduct of non-dominant firms). Type II errors are likely to induce more significant harm than Type I errors. The Commission is perfectly able to accurately and efficiently prohibit the anti-competitive conduct and keep Type II errors to a minimum. The possibility of some Type I errors should not prevent the Commission from having the ability to address anti-competitive conduct of non-dominant firms. Through a less rigid application of the dominance test the Commission may be able to reduce both Type I and Type II errors.

The Economic Advisory Group argued that a reduction in the role of separate assessments of dominance although will depart from the tradition of case law concerning Art. 82 of the Treaty, it will not depart from the legal norm itself.[27] Thus, the Commission could in the future cases, without

[27] EAGCP Report, 14.

departing from the essence of Article 82, allege that the anti-competitive conduct of the non-dominant firms may in some circumstances (ie differentiated products market, significant market share of the firm) harm consumer welfare and thus constitutes an infringement of Article 82. Due to the absence of such cases in the current case law, the Commission should notify the legal and business community of its new approach, so as to enhance legal certainty and encourage the dissemination of information about possible gap cases. The Economic Advisory Group correctly argued that greater flexibility of an effects-based approach need not reduce the predictability of competition policy.

Although this change in the Commission's approach is radical, it is necessary in order to prevent cases such *Rossignol*,[28] or to address the types of anti-competitive conduct that were evident in *Bayer* (and other cases analysed in the preceding sections) from escaping the Commission's assessment. We should also emphasize the fact that in five years, under the legislation on abuse of economic dependence, the Bundeskartellamt initiated more than one hundred proceedings, for abuse of purchasing power by major distributors.[29] According to the German competition authority's response to the ICN Report-ASBP, the Bundeskartellamt has examined 39 cases (beyond preliminary investigation) and three of them ended with a decision that the conduct violated antitrust rules. In France, 25 to 30 judgments have been delivered every year since 2001.[30] This number of cases on average is higher than the average number of decisions involving abuses of Article 82 or of equivalent national legislations.[31]

Thus, the corrective, and more importantly deterrence, impact of the ability of authorities to capture abusive conduct of non-dominant firms is likely to be higher and be illustrated in a larger number of cases than the number of authorities' decisions involving abusive conduct of dominant firms.

Conduct such as that addressed in these cases can also arise in the Commission's decisional practice. Some of these cases will relate to abuse of superior bargaining position/abuse of economic dependence and some of these cases will relate to other harmful conduct of non-dominant firms inducing consumer harm. One can only wonder on the number of cases that are not caught under the current EC legislation and the application of the concept of dominance in Article 82 cases.

[28] KZR 1/75, Rossignol, 20 November, 1975, WuW/E BGH, 1391.

[29] See further: I Roudard, 'The New French Legislation on Competition' [1989] 10(2) ECLR 205–232.

[30] In Korea, more than 2,380 cases were received, and corrective orders were imposed on 360 cases.

[31] Since 2001 there are about 16 decisions involving investigations pursuant to Article 82.

A. Enforcement Issues

The ability of the Commission to penalize conduct of non-dominant firms is likely to lead to an increased number of such complaints which will be very resource demanding. Thus, the Commission should have certain filters in order to deal with the cases that are likely to produce the biggest benefits for consumers. The Commission should have as its objective the welfare of consumers. In addition, the Commission should apply criteria in deciding which cases to take forward.

Six of the seven agencies which responded to the ICN questionnaire and have specific provisions for addressing abuse of superior bargaining position mentioned the probability of finding an alternative trade partner as one of the criteria. Five of the seven agencies identified the degree of trade dependence on the firm by the other, as well as the supply and demand forces of the product or service and difference in scale of business between the parties as relevant criteria for assessing such conduct.

The French authorities apply four criteria in deciding which abuse of economic dependence cases merit further investigation. The French criteria are (1) notoriety of the trading partner; (2) significance of its market share; (3) importance of the part of turnover achieved with this trading partner in the total turnover; and (4) difficulty to find alternative commercial partners offering similar commercial solutions.

For each complaint received which meets these four criteria, it will be assumed that it entails economic dependence. After substantiating the existence of economic dependence the authorities will examine whether there is an abuse and whether the abuse affects competition. Complaints which meet the 'economic dependence' and the 'abuse' criteria are likely to also have an adverse impact on competition and thus will be investigated further by the authorities. Since 1986, there have been between 40 and 50 complaints investigated which led to seven condemnation decisions. The Bundeskartellamt noted[32] that according to the German legislation all complaints need to be assessed. However, if a fundamental issue is involved it will surely take a case forward. In addition, if a particular conduct has ramifications which affect other undertakings/individuals in addition to the complainant, the Bundeskartellamt will open an investigation. Finally, the Bundeskartellamt added that the availability of resources will also be taken into account in deciding which cases to take forward.

Authorities should have some filtering criteria which will comprise of prioritization criteria and initial assessment criteria. Not all complaints lodged before the authorities will merit further investigation. As above-

[32] In a telephone conversation between Ioannis Kokkoris and Markus Lange, Head of the International Section of the Bundeskartellamt.

mentioned there are likely to be a significant number of complaints alleging abusive conduct of non-dominant firms. The authorities in order to be pragmatic in the enforcement of such legislation must be in a position to decide which complaints to take forward. The decision of initiating an investigation of a conduct will depend on the priorities of the authority as well as on an initial assessment of the harm resulting from the allegedly anti-competitive conduct of the non-dominant firm.

In the context of the application of section 5, Creighton et al argue[33] that *section 5 is in fact a good vehicle for what Congress intended—to define and proscribe forms of anti-competitive conduct, even if they are hard to analyze under existing Sherman Act precedents*. They add that in relation to section 5 of the FTC Act, the question to be considered is whether *the conduct at issue have the same effect, from an economic perspective, as the types of conduct that are subject to liability under the Sherman Act?* Similarly we can ask whether the anti-competitive conduct of a non-dominant undertaking has *the same effect, from an economic perspective, as the types of conduct that are subject to liability* under Article 82.

Similarly, FTC Commissioner Rosch argues that there must be some limiting principles on the application of section 5, whether the challenge is made under the 'unfair act or practice' prong of the statute (the abovementioned *N-Data*) or the 'unfair method of competition' prong (*N-Data*[34] and *Valassis*[35]).[36]

In *Ethyl*, the US court described an unfair method of competition as requiring at least some indicia of oppressiveness, such as (1) evidence of anti-competitive intent or purpose on the part of the producer charged; or (2) the absence of an independent legitimate business reason for its conduct.[37] In *Boise Cascade* the court argued that in the absence of per se illegal conduct, proof of actual or incipient anti-competitive effect is also required when the theory is that there is an unfair method of competition.[38]

Rosch added that it may be that the effect element of the claim can be inferred from clear evidence of anti-competitive intent (and lack of 'objective justification'). He adds though there must be some evidence, direct or circumstantial, of actual or incipient anti-competitive effect.[39]

[33] S Creighton et al, 'Some Thoughts About the Scope of Section 5', FTC Workshop on Section 5, 17 October 2008, www.ftc.gov.

[34] *In the Matter of Negotiated Data Solutions LLC*, FTC File No 051 0094 (23 January 2008).

[35] *In the Matter of Valassis Communications Inc* No 51-0008 (14 March 2006).

[36] See further: Welcoming Remarks of Thomas Rosch, FTC Workshop on Section 5, 17 October 2008, www.ftc.gov.

[37] *Ethyl*, 729 F.2d at 139.

[38] *Boise Cascade*, 630 F.2d at paragraph 582.

[39] Welcoming Remarks of Thomas Rosch, FTC Workshop on Section 5, 17 October 2008, www.ftc.gov.

The Commission and other national authorities should have prioritization criteria in order to decide which cases involving abusive conduct by non-dominant undertakings will be taken forward. Prioritization criteria should include the impact of the conduct on consumer welfare. This impact can be both direct and indirect effect. Direct effect will incorporate better value products for consumers in terms of price, quality service and other dynamic and non-dynamic factors. Indirect impact will incorporate the deterrence of firms to be involved in such conduct as well as the increased awareness of consumers of the likely anti-competitive conduct of non-dominant firms.

In addition, the authorities should take such cases forward in order to create the relevant case law precedence and avoid the need for more 'drastic' means of acquiring the ability to address anti-competitive conduct of non-dominant firms. Such 'innovative' precedents will also equip the authorities with expertise on dealing with such cases. Finally, the authorities may proceed with cases which 'fit' their policy strategy and meet their targets of enforcing competition legislation.

Enforcement of competition legislation against abusive conduct of non-dominant firms is likely to lead to appeals before the judicial authorities. Competition authorities should be prone to take this risk in order to achieve judicial 'seal of approval' of enforcement against abusive conduct of non-dominant firms. In the absence of legislative changes, the judicial 'seal of approval' will confirm the ability of the authorities to capture such conduct. Thus, authorities should not be risk averse (at least at the early stages) of enforcing competition legislation against such conduct. As I mentioned above, it is my firm belief that such risk is acceptable and should be taken by the Commission and other competition authorities in order to advance the enforcement of competition legislation and to improve competition policy.

We can depict the weight of the various prioritization criteria using the following ratio:

$$\frac{\text{Risk} \qquad \text{Resources}}{\text{Impact} \qquad \text{Significance}}$$

The ideal result for a competition authority is for this ratio to be equal to one. A ratio higher than one implies higher risk and more resource intensive cases with small impact and significance. Although competition authorities may wish to keep this ratio at low risk and resource needs but high impact and significance cases, such a ratio may imply underestimation of risk and overstretching of resources. It may also indicate a risk-averse approach adopted by the authority. Lower risk cases are likely to be

proportional to the precedential significance of a case. Cases which have set important precedents in the history of competition enforcement are cases raising controversial issues that were addressed and given the judicial seal of approval.

In addressing conduct of non-dominant firms the authorities should try to maintain this ratio at one or ideally, and as case law on such conduct progresses, lower than one. The authorities should be prepared though at the initial stages of addressing such conduct to have this ratio at higher than one, until the 'learning curve' of the authorities and the courts adapt to the need as well as the method of addressing such conduct.

In addition, competition authorities should have criteria to assess the likely harm resulting from the conduct under investigation.[40] Initial assessment criteria to determine whether an allegedly anti-competitive conduct of a non-dominant firm should be investigated further should include, inter alia:

- **Relative market shares.**
  The assessment of relative market shares draws a different picture than the assessment of individual market shares. The relative market shares may be an initial rough indication of the competitive constraints that each firm is imposing on the other incumbents.[41] The importance of the market share as an indication of market power depends on the level relative to that of the nearest competitor as well as on factors tending to entrench the market position of the firm (eg differentiation).
- **Degree of differentiation in the market.**
  If the products are differentiated, so that products sold by different participants in the market are not perfect substitutes for one another, an anti-competitive conduct by the second biggest firm in a market with differentiated products may diminish competition by enabling it to profit by this conduct, without at the same time incurring substantial switching of customers from its products to rivals' products.
- **Diversion between the firms' products.**[42]
  As mentioned above, what should be taken into account in differentiated

[40] Annex 2 provides a list of the most important criteria that are used in the assessment of single firm dominance/substantial market power in a number of jurisdictions that responded to ICN questionnaires. These general criteria are also important in assessing whether a non-dominant firm can induce harm on consumer welfare by adopting anti-competitive conduct.

[41] A more concrete analysis would need the calculation of diversion ratios. Market shares must be used with caution in drawing conclusions. In markets with homogeneous products, market shares can be used as proxies for diversion ratios.

[42] The accurate calculation of diversion ratios at the initial stages of the assessment is likely to be difficult and will depend on the availability of data. If such data are available, calculation of the diversion ratio is likely to provide an accurate account not only of the non-dominant firm's market power but also of the realistic use of alternative sources.

product markets where firms produce substitute products is the diversion ratio,[43] which will indicate the diversion of sales from the products of one of the firm to the other firms' products, in case of an anti-competitive conduct by that firm. This diversion ratio is calculated by looking at customers' choices if they switch away from a firm that adopts the anti-competitive conduct (eg increases its price).

- **Alternative sources of supply of the product.**
  Alternative sources of supplies may prove sufficient in mitigating any anti-competitive conduct from the non-dominant firm. The adequacy of these alternatives will depend on the degree of differentiation of the product as well as on possible capacity constraints that the incumbents in the market may face. If the competitors of the non-dominant firm are able to compensate for the anti-competitive conduct (the cessation of supply), the conduct may not lead to any consumer harm. Even in markets characterized by homogeneous products and capacity constraints faced by the incumbents, an anti-competitive conduct of any the non-dominant undertaking will not be mitigated by reaction from other incumbents if they are not able to increase capacity in order to absorb the switching of demand emanating from the anti-competitive conduct of the non-dominant firm. Thus, in Cournot markets, if there are no capacity constraints, the incumbent firms will react to the anti-competitive conduct of any the non-dominant undertaking, mitigating thus the adverse impact on the market.

  In the case of a market with differentiated products though, as is likely to be the case in gap cases, capacity constraints are not so important, as in markets with homogeneous products, since the reaction of the rival firms is unlikely to significantly mitigate the anti-competitive conduct of the non-dominant undertaking, in contrast to the case of the Cournot type of competition, where, since the products are homogeneous, the non-dominant firm's conduct can be easily mitigated.
- **Impact on consumers.**
  The Guidance paper seems to adopt an approach, advocating that an anti-competitive conduct is not prohibited unless it entails significant consumer harm, after an off-setting of the harm to consumers against the (mainly short-term) benefits for the consumers has been effected.[44]

[43] The closeness of substitution between products does not only depend on the degree of differentiation of these products, but also on factors such as capacity constraints and barriers to entry and expansion.

[44] See also EAGCP Report, http://ec.europa.eu/comm/competition/publications/studies/eagcp july 21 05.pdf. As stated therein: 'An economics-based approach to the application of article 82 implies that the assessment of each specific case will not be undertaken on the basis of the form that a particular business practice takes (for example, exclusive dealing, tying, etc) but rather will be based on the assessment of the anti-competitive effects generated by business behaviour. This implies that competition authorities will need to identify a competitive harm,

Depending on whether the product of the non-dominant undertaking is homogeneous or differentiated, the impact on consumers will vary since their ability to find alternative sources of supply will vary.

- **Lack of objective justification.**
  Where an undertaking has been found to have infringed Article 82, the undertaking can defend its conduct by arguing that it is '*objectively justified*'.

  Should the undertaking succeed in this defence, the conduct will not amount to an abuse.[45] This concept, developed by the ECJ and the Commission, distinguishes abusive conduct from that which is pursued as a matter of legitimate commercial policy. However, this defence cannot apply to conduct whose aim is to weaken competition. In addition, it involves an element of proportionality.[46]

A dynamic, rather than static, analysis of the market structure will allow the Commission to perform an accurate assessment of the anti-competitive conduct of non-dominant firms. Such a dynamic analysis will incorporate a number of other structural factors beyond market shares and market concentration that can affect the degree of intra-market rivalry in a market. Such dynamic analysis would entail the assessment of the extent of intra-market rivalry which will depend on whether firms' cost structures are very similar or not, and how low-cost firms utilize this advantage. In addition the degree of spare capacity in a market and the ease with which existing capacity can be expanded are two additional factors that may influence the degree of intra-market rivalry. Furthermore, the ownership and organizational form of firms might also affect the degree of intra-market rivalry.

and assess the extent to which such a negative effect on consumers is potentially outweighed by efficiency gains. The identification of competitive harm requires spelling out a consistent business behaviour based on sound economics and supported by facts and empirical evidence. Similarly, efficiencies and how they are passed on to consumers should be properly justified on the basis of economic analysis and grounded on the facts of each case.'

[45] Rousseva (2006) argues that the scope of objective justification is not entirely clear but it has generally been accepted that the objective justification refers to public policy concerns or other objective factors, such as crisis in the industry, which force undertakings to deviate from their normal course of conduct. She conducts an analysis of important precedents and adds that Community Courts understand the concept of objective justification to include only two types of considerations: (i) purely objective factors beyond the control of undertakings (not only dominant ones) which prevent those undertakings from carrying out their normal course of conduct; and (ii) public policy considerations which are generally of a non-economic nature but in particular circumstances, for example where there is a need to provide efficient service to the public, may be given an economic dimension. See further: Rousseva E, 'The Concept of 'Objective Justification' of an Abuse of a Dominant Position: Can it help to Modernise the Analysis under Article 82 EC?' [2005] 2(2) Comp L Rev.

[46] C Stothers (2001) 'Refusal to Supply as Abuse of a Dominant Position: Essential Facilities in the European Union' [2001] 7 ECLR 256, 260.

As mentioned above, markets with a similar structure can display different degrees of intra-market rivalry as a result of many factors. Non-structural factors that might affect the level of intra-market rivalry can include, for example, the different ability of, and capacity for, firms to innovate; the objectives and culture of the firms in the market, their views on the future development of the market and on the appropriate strategies to meet those developments; the history of pricing behaviour in the market and the extent to which transparent prices are available in the market.[47]

The assessment of some of the abovementioned criteria (eg objective justification) may necessitate significant resources. In cases where they are clearly satisfied (eg existence of objective justification), the authorities will be able to reject a complaint at an early stage of the assessment process. In other cases, resources may need to be devoted in order to examine whether these criteria are satisfied. The devotion of these resources to such an investigation may be necessary in order to ensure that all conduct of non-dominant firms inducing consumer harm is captured.

The Commission or a national competition authority will need to consider the desired portfolio of cases and select priority sectors as well as policy objectives. Some relevant considerations include whether enforcement action is the most effective one to stop the infringement as well as the possibility of another regulator or another legislative tool to address the allegedly anti-competitive conduct. The opportunities for private enforcement should also be taken into consideration. Private enforcement for such claims may also be successful in addressing such conduct. However, the authorities are likely to be in a better position, as regards resources and the focus of competition policy, in dealing with such issues.

In addition the competition authority could assess the consumer harm that arises and thus the resulting benefit from intervention (product and geographic extent of the alleged conduct, firms involved etc.). The authority's action against abuses by non-dominant firms will have a deterrent effect on other non-dominant firms that may be abusing their market power. The same deterrent effect will dissuade firms in general from adopting anti-competitive conduct. Aggravating and mitigating factors can also play a role in choosing to address a particular conduct.[48] Finally, the precedential value of addressing the conduct can also be very important in shaping the future case law related to anti-competitive conduct of non-dominant firms. Since, the ability of the Commission to address such conduct can be easily derived through CFI/ECJ case law, the precedential value of such

[47] See further: *Market Investigation References: Competition Commission Guidelines*, www.competition-commission.org.uk.

[48] For a list of such factors, see further: *Competition Prioritisation Framework*, Office of Fair Trading, www.oft.gov.uk.

cases is of immense importance. Finally the demands in resources and the likelihood of success should also be taken into account.

The resources required for dealing with the likely large number of allegations and complaints are surely significant. However, the filtering of the complaints through effective prioritization and assessment criteria and investigating fully the ones with the highest precedential value which induce the biggest consumer welfare harm, will ensure that the Commission and national competition authorities will be in a position to enforce competition legislation in a more effective and accurate way and address all types of anti-competitive conduct.

Conclusion

This book has addressed the gap in the enforcement of Article 82 and in some of the relevant national provisions. It also dealt with the inability of the Commission as well as that of some Member States to capture conduct that relates to abuse of superior bargaining position/abuse of economic dependence.

Consumer harm induced by anti-competitive conduct of non-dominant firms can arise in markets where firms compete with differentiated products and the products of the non-dominant rivals are not close substitutes. Similarly, they may arise if competitors are not close competitors because of their geographic location. In the case where products are differentiated based on brand image, technical specifications, quality, or level of service, customers often prefer different suppliers. If the incumbents can alter their product line and become close substitutes to the allegedly non-dominant firm, the induced harm from the non-dominant firm's anti-competitive conduct will be mitigated. Furthermore, in case competitors are located within close proximity, even if the relevant geographic market is relatively large, competition can be localized and the geographic location of suppliers will constitute a significant competitive factor.

In general, if there are a number of alternative suppliers to whom a significant number of customers are willing to turn, the threat of losing these customers may be adequate to place a constraint on the non-dominant firm. However, product differentiation as well as the inability of competitors to react by either increasing output (if spare capacity is limited), or repositioning in order to place a constraint on the non-dominant firm, is conducive to consumer harm arising from the non-dominant firm's anti-competitive conduct.[1]

Some EU jurisdictions apply the concept of abuse of superior bargaining position/abuse of economic dependence in order to address anti-competitive conduct of non-dominant firms. The scope of application differs amongst these countries (eg only on buyer side, grocery sector). The Commission though does not apply this concept at all. It risks thus not addressing anti-competitive conduct of non-dominant firms which induces consumer harm and would be addressed by the national legislation of Member States. Although the ability of Member States to apply such

[1] Concerns of consumer harm induced by anti-competitive conduct of non-dominant firms can also arise if the suppliers' capacities are the main driver of competition, rather than product differentiation, and competitors would be unlikely to react to an increased demand arising from the adoption of an anti-competitive conduct by the non-dominant firm by increasing output due to capacity constraints they may be facing.

stricter rules compared to Article 82 is acknowledged in Regulation 1/2003, the Commission does not apply such rules.

Thus, the gap in the application of the dominance test has resulted from the dependence of a finding of a dominant firm on the market share of the firm. As the above analysis illustrated, applying the concept of dominance in that way means that a non-dominant firm in a differentiated market can adopt anti-competitive conduct and not be deterred by the possible application of Article 82.[2]

The Economic Advisory Group argued that it seems more appropriate to have the implementation of the Treaty itself focus on the abuses and to treat the assessment of dominance in this context.[3] Although a reduction in the role of separate assessments of dominance will depart from the tradition of case law concerning Article 82 of the Treaty, it will not depart from the legal norm itself.[4] Thus, the Commission could in future cases, without departing from the essence of Article 82, assess whether the anti-competitive conduct of non-dominant firms may harm consumer harm and thus constitute an infringement of Article 82.

The Commission needs to address the abuse of superior bargaining position/economic dependence, as is currently done by Member States and advocated by the ICN. In addition, the Commission must be capable of addressing the conduct of non-dominant firms. By addressing such conduct the Commission will ensure that it captures all conduct that leads to harm to consumers and to competition in general.

According to Regulation 1/2003:[5]

> If the competition rules are to be applied consistently and, at the same time, the network is to be managed in the best possible way, it is essential to retain the rule that the competition authorities of the Member States are automatically relieved of their competence if the Commission initiates its own proceedings. Where a competition authority of a Member State is already acting on a case and the Commission intends to initiate proceedings, it should endeavour to do so as soon as possible. Before initiating proceedings, the Commission should consult the national authority concerned.

[2] Lucey (2006) referring to Regulation 1/2003 argues that Article 3 is not clearly defined in terms of scope. In particular, the meaning of 'national competition law' is not set. Member States' insistence on exceptions to allow the application of national laws created a text with uncertain boundaries. The scope of the national laws which predominantly pursue an objective different from that of Articles 81 and 82 will be crucial for litigants, seeking to void an agreement permitted by Article 81. See further: M C Lucey, 'Unforeseen consequences of Article 3 of EU Regulation 1/2003' [2006] 27(10) 558–563, 563.

[3] EAGCP Report, 15.

[4] EAGCP Report, 14.

[5] Recital 17.

Having consumer welfare as the Commission's standard, the Commission should ensure that it captures such conduct, especially in differentiated markets where there may not be significant switching from the second biggest firm to other incumbents, thus bestowing the non-dominant firm with market power.

In addition, relaxing the 'assessment' of when a firm can adopt harmful conduct to consumers and when this conduct should be subject to competition legislation will ensure a reduction of both Type I and Type II errors in the enforcement of Article 82, rather than over enforcement and more importantly ensure a more accurate and effective enforcement of competition legislation.

Drawing a parallel with the application in the USA of section 5 of the FTC Act, the fact that the Sherman Act cannot address some types of harmful conduct does not always mean that the conduct is no longer harmful. We should echo some of Commissioner Rosch's[6] thoughtful questions that he poses as regards the application of section 5 of the FTC Act.

- Should enforcement of Section 5 be confined to conduct that the Commission also finds does not violate the Sherman Act (or the Clayton Act)?
- Should conduct that cannot be shown to injure the competitive process ever be considered an unfair method of competition, and, if so, when?
- What should be the practical, workable boundaries susceptible to coherent application?
- How can unfair methods of competition under Section 5 be defined to avoid capturing benign or pro-competitive conduct while allowing for sufficient guidance and predictability for business?
- Are there some universal limiting principles? If not, what limiting principles may be applicable?

Similar questions are equally valid for the gap in the application of Article 82 and we have already raised such questions throughout this book.

- Should Article 82 apply to conduct of non-dominant firms?
- Should conduct of non-dominant firms that does not induce consumer harm be liable to an Article 82 infringement?
- Should any conduct of non-dominant firms constitute an abuse pursuant to Article 82?
- How can the allegations against conduct of non-dominant firms prevent any inhibition of innovation and R&D?

[6] Welcoming Remarks of Thomas Rosch, FTC Workshop on Section 5, 17 October 2008, www.ftc.gov.

The answer to the question whether Article 82 should apply to non-dominant conduct should be answered in the affirmative. The focus of the investigations should be conduct of non-dominant firms that induces consumer harm. By accurately enforcing Article 82 to such conduct, any inhibition of innovation and R&D is likely to be minimal. The more legal certainty that the Commission and the CFI/ECJ (through their approval of cases against the conduct of non-dominant firms) can infiltrate in the legal and business community, the less inhibiting is the enforcement of Article 82 going to be for the innovation and R&D of non-dominant firms. As mentioned above, the possibility of some Type I errors should not prevent the Commission from having the ability to address anti-competitive conduct of non-dominant firms. Through a less rigid application of the dominance test the Commission may be able to reduce both Type I and Type II errors.

Answering these questions will ensure a competition enforcement system where conduct significantly harming consumer welfare will be penalized irrespective of whether the conduct is attributed to a dominant or a non-dominant firm. The conduct that should be subject to sanctions is the conduct of firms enjoying market power, and as we illustrated in this book, market power does not necessitate the highest market share as seems to be the practical treatment of market power by the Commission and the Courts.

We should reiterate ECJ's definition of dominance in *Hoffmann-La Roche*[7] where the ECJ defined the notion of dominance as 'a position of economic strength enjoyed by an undertaking, which enables it to behave to an appreciable extent independently of its competitors, its customers and ultimately of consumers'. This independence that the ECJ gives emphasis in its definition of dominance does not necessitate the highest market share in a market. It necessitates the ability to adopt anti-competitive conduct without a credible threat of customer reaction (eg switching to the products of rivals) that would prevent the adoption of such conduct. In such market structures, that are analysed herein, conduct of non-dominant firms can induce consumer harm and should become subject to Article 82.

This book has clearly illustrated the gap in the enforcement of Article 82. The Commission is unable to capture the conduct that not only the Member States can address with legislation on abuse of superior bargaining position/abuse of economic dependence but conduct that the US FTC can address by applying section 5 of the FTC Act. The Commission following some of the analysis and means identified herein should attempt to address this gap and improve the accuracy in the enforcement of Article 82.

[7] Case 85/76, *Hoffmann-La Roche & Co AG v Commission* [1979] ECR I-461, § 38.

A. Further Areas of Research

Further areas of research can include the examination of cases where the Commission examined a possible abusive conduct by an undertaking but did not sustain the allegation on the basis that the undertaking was not found to be dominant. If it can be proved that the conduct of this undertaking was harming consumer welfare to a significant extent then the Commission ought to be able to address it with sanctions. Unfortunately the Commission does not publish detailed decisions where it states that an abuse has not been substantiated.[8] In addition, it would be interesting to assess whether the cases that have been found in the Member States that have the ability to capture anti-competitive conduct of non-dominant firms could have been caught by the Commission.

The identification of such cases would illustrate the consumer welfare harm that the Commission is not able to capture due to its inability to address the gap in the application of Article 82. This identification could even incorporate the detailed types of conduct of non-dominant firms that are likely to induce significant consumer harm.[9]

Additionally, future research could focus on the issue of the cost, the availability and proportionality of remedies to rectify harm in the equilibrium status quo. Such research would provide interesting insights in the means of rectifying anti-competitive conduct of non-dominant firms. A relevant factor will also be the ease of monitoring and enforcing compliance notwithstanding the possibility of setting a compliance programme. The effectiveness of any remedy may be reduced if elaborate, and possibly costly, monitoring and compliance programmes are required.

Ideally though, the Commission should ensure that it has the means to address such conduct and can use its discretion and expertise to identify proportionate remedies. In imposing the remedies the Commission should ensure it does not 'over-correct' and thus dampen innovation or the competitive process in general. Drawing a parallel from the enforcement of section 5 of the FTC Act, according to Creighton et al,[10] section 5 (which applies to conduct that is beyond Sherman Act applicability) should not, be allowed to impose antitrust liability for conduct that does not threaten these fundamental principles of antitrust—that is, the latitude that Congress built into section 5 should not be used to sacrifice efficient behavior for insignificant or illusory increases in consumer welfare or to shield competitors from the

[8] Although following Regulation 1/2003, the Commission can publish such decisions.

[9] In addition, the possibility of anti-competitive conduct by non-dominant firms in dynamic oligopolies with free entry and the impact of such conduct on long-term consumer harm also merit further research.

[10] S Creighton et al, 'Some Thoughts About the Scope of Section 5' FTC Workshop on Section 5, 17 October 2008, www.ftc.gov, 2.

rigors of efficient competition. Thus, the application of Article 82 to the anti-competitive conduct of non-dominant firms should ensure that undertakings are able to adopt strategies in the market without being concerned with possible allegations of anti-competitive conduct and with the ensuing remedies by the Commission.

Finally, a very interesting area for future research is the prioritization criteria that an authority should apply in assessing whether the conduct of a non-dominant firm merits further investigation. Accurate prioritization criteria will ensure that the authorities will be effective in capturing anti-competitive conduct of non-dominant firms that induce significant consumer harm, while at the same time not devoting significant resources on investigations of conduct of non-dominant undertakings which do not lead to significant consumer harm.

Commissioner Kroes in her speech of 23 September 2005 to the Fordham Corporate Law Institute[11] mentioned that:

> In order to conclude that a company has substantial market power one must conduct a detailed analysis of key issues such as the market position of the allegedly dominant company, the market position of competitors, barriers to expansion and entry, and the market position of buyers.
>
> This means that I consider that high market shares are not—on their own—sufficient to conclude that a dominant position exists. Market share presumptions can result in an excessive focus on establishing the exact market shares of the various market participants. A pure market share focus risks failing to take proper account of the degree to which competitors can constrain the behaviour of the allegedly dominant company. That is not to say that market shares have no significance. They may provide an indication of dominance—and sometimes a very strong indication—but in the end a full economic analysis of the overall situation is necessary.

Commissioner Kroes argues that *a pure market share focus risks failing to take proper account of the degree to which competitors can constrain the behaviour of the allegedly dominant company*. Such a focus also fails to take proper account of the degree to which competitors of the dominant firm can adopt abusive anti-competitive conduct as well. We should emphasize here that, irrespective of Commissioner Kroes' arguments, there has

[11] N Kroes, 'Preliminary Thoughts on Policy Review of Article 82' speech given on 23 September 2005at the Fordham Corporate Law Institute New York. http://europe.eu/rapid/pressReleasesAction.do.?reference=SPEECH/05/537&format=HTML&aged=0&language=EV&guiLanguage=en

never been either a Commission decision or a CFI/ECJ judgment that alleges or sustains a finding of an abuse by a non-dominant firm.

The gap in the application of Article 82 must be rectified in order to ensure effective enforcement of competition legislation on abusive conduct of non-dominant firms which are likely to induce consumer harm.

Annex 1

REPORT PREPARED BY THE ICN UNILATERAL CONDUCT WORKING GROUP (ICN REPORT)

	Countries objectives	Ensuring an effective competitive process as a goal and/or a means	Promote consumer welfare	Maximize efficiency	Ensure economic freedom	Ensure a level playing field for SMEs	Promote fairness and equality	Promote consumer choice	Achieve market integration	Facilitate privatization and market liberalization	Promote competitiveness in international markets
1	Australia	X[c]	X	X		X			X		
2	Brazil	X[a]	X	X	X						
3	Bulgaria	X[a]	X		X		X				
4	Canada	X[b]	X	X		X		X			X
5	Chile	X[a]									
6	Czech Republic	X[a]			X						
7	European Union	X[b]	X	X					X		
8	France	X[a]	X	X	X		X				
9	Germany	X[a]	X	X	X	X					
10	Hungary	X[b]	X	X							
11	Ireland	X[b]	X					X			
12	Israel	X[a]	X		X						
13	Italy	X[b]	X		X						
14	Jamaica	X[c]	X	X			X	X			
15	Japan	X[a]	X				X				
16	Jersey	X[b]	X	X	X						
17	Korea	X[b]	X		X	X	X				
18	Latvia	X[b]	X					X			
19	Mexico	X[a]	X	X	X						
20	Netherlands	X[b]	X								
21	New Zealand	X[b]	X	X					X	X	

	Countries objectives	Ensuring an effective competitive process as a goal and/or a means	Promote consumer welfare	Maximize efficiency	Ensure economic freedom	Ensure a level playing field for SMEs	Promote fairness and equality	Promote consumer choice	Achieve market integration	Facilitate privatization and market liberalization	Promote competitiveness in international markets
22	Pakistan		X	X	X						
23	Romania	X[b]	X								
24	Russia	X[a]	X	X	X				X	X	
25	Singapore	X[c]		X							
26	Slovak Republic	X[b]	X								
27	South Africa	X[b]	X	X		X	X	X			X
28	Sweden	X[b]	X								
29	Switzerland	X[a]	X	X	X	X					
30	Turkey	X[a]	X	X		X					
31	Ukraine	X[a]	X	X							
32	United Kingdom	X[c]	X	X							
33	United States	X[b]	X	X							
	Total	32	30	20	13	7	6	5	4	2	2

* 33 agencies answered Part A of the Questionnaire relevant to Objectives.

a. 13 agencies cite ensuring an effective competitive process as a goal.

b. 15 agencies cite ensuring an effective competitive process as both a goal and a means. As noted in Section I of the report, this includes the 5 agencies that can be inferred to fall within this category.

c. 4 agencies cite ensuring an effective competitive process exclusively as a means to achieve other goals.

Annex 2

REPORT PREPARED BY THE ICN UNILATERAL CONDUCT WORKING GROUP (ICN REPORT)

Annex C:
Of the criteria that you use to assess single-firm dominance/substantial market power which are the most important criteria?

	Market share of the firm and its competitors	Barriers to entry or expansion	Market position and behavior of	Buyer power	Durability of market power
Australia					
Brazil	1	1	1		
Bulgaria	1	1			
Canada	1	1			
Chile		1			
Czech Republic	1				
European Com	1	1	1	1	
France	1	1	1		
Germany	1	1	1		
Hungary	1	1	1		
India	1		1		
Ireland	1	1	1	1	1
Italy	1				
Israel	1	1			
jamaica	1	1	1		1
Japan					
Jersey					
Korea	1				
Latvia	1	1			
Mexico	1	1	1		
Netherlands	1	1			1
New Zealand		1	1		
Pakistan	1				
Romania	1	1		1	
Russia	1	1			1
Singapore	1	1		1	
Slovakia	1	1			
South Africa	1				
Spain	1	1			
Sweden	1	1			
Switzerland	1	1	1	1	
Turkey	1	1			
United Kingdom					
Ukraine		1			
United States					
Total	27	24	11	5	4

Annex 3

REPORT PREPARED BY THE ICN UNILATERAL CONDUCT WORKING GROUP (ICN REPORT)

Annex E
Stages at which the competition authority can intervene
1 = Yes, 0 =No

	Under your general competition law governing unilateral conduct, at which stage(s) can your competition agency intervene against potentially abusive unilateral conduct?			Does your competition law enable the competition agency to intervene against unilateral conduct at a level below the dominance/SMP threshold?
	If dominance/ SMP is present	Acquisition or creation of dominance/ SMP	Attempt to acquire or create dominance/ SMP	
Australia	1	0	0	0
Brazil	1	1	1	1
Bulgaria	1	0	0	0
Canada	1	0	0	0
Chile	1	1	1	1
Czech Republic	1	0	0	0
European Com	1	0	0	0
France	1	0	0	1
Germany	1	0	0	1
Hungary	1	0	0	0
India	1	1	1	0
Ireland	1	0	0	0
Italy	1	0	0	0
Israel	1	0	0	1
Jamaica	1	0	0	1
Japan	n.a.	n.a.	n.a.	1
Jersey	1	1	0	0
Korea	1	1	1	1
Latvia	1	0	0	0
Mexico	1	0	0	0
Netherlands	1	0	0	0
New Zealand	1	0	0	0
Pakistan	1	1	0	1
Romania	1	0	0	0
Russia	1	1	1	1
Singapore	1	0	0	0
Slovakia	1	0	0	0
South Africa	1	0	0	0
Spain	1	0	0	1
Sweden	1	1	0	0
Switzerland	1	0	0	0
Turkey	1	0	0	0
United Kingdom	1	0	0	0
Ukraine	1	0	0	0
United States	1	1	1	0

Annex 4

Appendix C of the ICN Kyoto-ASBP.
Jurisdictions with Abuse of Superior Bargaining Position legislations.

	Criteria under Superior Bargaining Position Provisions						Effects	Sanctions/ Remedies						Countervailing Power	Who Enforces?		Number of Cases				Private Enforcement
	a	b	c	d	e	f		g	h	i	j	k	l		Competition Authority	Other	m	n	o	p	
1. Austria								X							X	X					X
2. France	X	X	X	X				X	X				X		X	X	25-30/ 1 yr				X
3. Germany	X	X	X	X			X	X	X					X	X		39	3	31	5	X
4. Italy	X	X	X	X					X					X	X	X					X
5. Japan	X	X	X	X		X		X				X			X		98	12	10		X
6. Korea	X	X	X	X				X	X	X	X	X	X		X		2,382	360			
7. Slovak Rep.		X							X							X					X
Total	5	6	5	5	0	1	1	5	5	1	1	2	2	2	6	4	(2,519)	375	41	5	6

a. Degree of dependence
b. Probability of finding an alternative
c. Supply and demand forces
d. Differences in scale of business
e. Harm to consumer welfare
f. Other

g. Cease/desist (prohibition)
h. Fines
i. Imprisonment
j. Surcharge
k. Public announcement
l. Other

m. Reviewed
n. Violation
o. No violation
p. Settlement

Bibliography

BOOKS—ARTICLES—LEGISLATION

WJ Adams & JL Yellen, 'Commodity Bundling and the Burden of Monopoly' [1976] 90 Q J Econ 475.

C Ahlborn, D Evans, J Padilla, 'The Antitrust Economics of Tying: a Farewell to Per Se Illegality' [2004] The Antitrust Bulletin/Spring–Summer 287.

P Akman, 'To Abuse, or Not to Abuse: Discrimination Between Consumers' (2007) EL Rev 32(4), 492–512.

P Andrews, 'Is Meeting Competition a Defence to Predatory Pricing?—The Irish Sugar Decision Suggests a New Approach' [1998] ECLR 49.

M Armstrong and J Vickers, 'Price Discrimination, Competition and Regulation' [1993] 41 Journal of Industrial Economics.

M Armstrong, 'Recent Developments in the Economics of Price Discrimination' October 2005 Working Paper, http://129.3.20.41/eps/io/papers/0511/0511004.pdf.

JP Azevedo, M Walker, 'Dominance: Meaning and Measurement', [2001] CRA Competition Policy Discussion Papers 1–8, available from www.crai.co.uk.

JP Azevedo, M Walker, 'Dominance: Meaning and Measurement' [2002] ECLR 23(7) 363–367.

J Baker and T Bresnahan, 'The Gains from Merger or Collusion in Product Differentiated Industries' [1985] Journal of Industrial Economics 33, 427–444.

D Balto, 'A Section 5 Enforcement Agenda That Even Bill O'Reilly Could Love', FTC Workshop on Section 5, 17 October 2008, www.ftc.gov.

R Bechtold and U Denzel in I Kokkoris, *Competition Cases from the European Union* (Sweet and Maxwell, London, 2007).

S Bishop, P Marsden, Editorial, 'The Article 82 Discussion Paper: A Missed Opportunity' [2006] European Competition Journal, 1.

S Bishop and M Walker, *The Economics of EC Competition Law: Concepts, Application and Measurement* (2nd edn, 2002).

WS Bowman, 'Tying Arrangements and the Leverage Problem' [1957] 67 Yale LR19.

R Brenkers, F Verboven, 'Market Definition with Differentiated Products—Lessons from the Car Market' (2005) http://www.cepr.org/pubs/dps/DP5249.asp.

L Cabral, 'Introduction to Industrial Organization' (The MIT Press, Cambridge Massachusetts, 2000) 72–75.

P Callol, P Pignatelli, 'Spain: General—Competition Enforcement' [2005] ECLR, 26(5), N71–72.

J Carbajo, D Meza, D Seidmann, 'A Strategic Motivation for Commodity Bundling' [1990] 38 The Journal of Industrial Economics 283.

D Carlton, 'A General Analysis of Exlusionary Conduct and Refusal to Deal—Why Aspen and Kodak Are Misguided,' [2001] NBER Working Book No 8105, www.nber.org/papers/w8105.

D Carlton & M Waldman, 'The Strategic Use of Tying to Preserve and Create Market Power in Evolving Industries' [2002] 33 Rand J Econ 194.

Y Chen, 'Equilibrium Product Bundling' [1997] 70 J Bus 85.

Z Chen, T Ross & WT Stanbury, 'Refusals to Deal and Aftermarkets' [1998] 13 Review of Industrial Organization 131.

J Church and R Ware, *Industrial Organization Strategic Approach* (McGraw-Hill, Singapore, 2000).

Communication from the Commission concerning certain aspects of the treatment of competition cases resulting from the expiry of the ECSC Treaty [2002] OJ C152/5, [2002] 5 CMLR 1036, Section 2: http://europa.eu.int/eur-lex/pri/en/oj/dat/2002/c_152/c_15220020626en 00050012.pdf.

CJ Cook and CS Kerse (2000), *E.C. Merger Control* (3rd edn, Sweet and Maxwell, London).

CP Correia, P Pinheiro, 'Portugal: Exploitation of Economic Dependence' [2001] ECLR 22(8), N117–119.

Council Regulation (EC) No 139/2004 of 20 January 2004 on the control of concentrations between undertakings (the EC Merger Regulation), (Recast ECMR) [2004] OJ L 24, 1–22.

Council Regulation (EEC) 4064/89 of 21 December 1989 on the control of concentrations between undertakings, [1989] OJ L395/1, corrigendum [1990] OJ L257/14.

P Craig and G De Burca, *EU Law—Text, Cases and Materials* (3rd edn, 2003).

D Crane, 'Multiproduct Discounting: A Myth of Nonprice Predation' [2005] 72 U Chi L Rev 27.

S Creighton et al, 'Some Thoughts About the Scope of Section 5' FTC Workshop on Section 5, 17 October 2008, www.ftc.gov.

KJ Cseres, 'The Controversies of the Consumer Welfare Standard' [2007] Competition Law Review, vol 3 issue 2.

F Dethmers, N Dodoo, 'The Abuse of Hoffmann-La Roche: the Meaning of Dominance under EC Competition Law' [2006] ECLR 27(10), 537–549.

A Dixit, 'A Model of Duopoly Suggesting a Theory of Entry Barriers' [1979] Bell Journal of Economics 10, 20–32.

I Dobbs, P Richards, 'Output restriction as a measure of market power' [2005] ECLR, 26(10), 572–580.

B Doherty, 'Just What Are Essential Facilities?' [2001] 38 CMLR 397.

EC Competition Policy Newsletter, Preserving and Promoting Competition: A European Response' (2006) – Number 2 – Summer.

T Eilmansberger, 'How to Distinguish Good From Bad Competition Under Article 82 EC: In Search of Clearer and More Coherent Standards for Anti-competitive Abuses' [2005] CMLR (PP) 129.

T Eilsmanberger, 'Dominance—The Lost Child? How Effects Based Rules Could and Should Change Analysis' [2006] European Competition Journal 15–29.

D Elliott, 'What is an Excessive Price?' [2007] Comp LI, 6(8), 13–15.

European Commission Notice Guidelines on the Application of Article 81(3) [2004] OJ C101.

D Evans & J Padilla, Designing Antitrust Rules for Assessing Unilateral Practices: A Neo – Chicago Approach [2005] 72 U Chi L Rev 73.

J Faull and A Nikpay, *The EC Law of Competition* (Oxford University Press, 2007).

First report of the activities of the Conseil de la Concurrence for 1987, at XXII.

K Fjell, L Sorgard, 'How to Test for Abuse of Dominance' [2006] European Competition Journal, July.

A Foyer, 'Section 5 as Bridge Towards Convergence', FTC Workshop on Section 5, 17 October 2008, www.ftc.gov.

M Furse, 'Article 82, Microsoft and bundling, or "The Half Monti"' [2004] Comp LJ, 3(3), 169–178.

M Gal, 'Below-cost price alignment: meeting or beating competition? The France Telecom case' [2007] ECLR , 28(6), 382–391.

D Geradin, N Petit, 'Price discrimination under EC competition law: another antitrust doctrine in search of limiting principles?' [2006] JCLE, 2(3), 479–531.

D Geradin, M Rato, 'Excessive pricing: in reply' [2006] Comp LI, 5(10), 3–5.

D Gerard, 'Price Discrimination under Article 82(c) EC: Clearing up the Ambiguities' in (July 2005) Global Competition Law Centre Research Papers on Article 82 EC.

H Gilliams, 'Modernisation: From Policy to Practice' [2003] EL Rev 28(4), 451–474.

M Glader, S Larsen, 'Article 82: excessive pricing' [2006] Comp LI, 5(7), 3–5.

L Gormsen, 'Article 82 EC: Where are we coming from and where are we going to?' [2006] Competition Law Review, vol 2, issue 2, March 2006.

M Gravengaard, 'The Meeting Competition Defence Principle—a Defence for Price Discrimination and Predatory Pricing?' [2006] ECLR 27(12), 658–677.

Guidance on the Commission's Enforcement Priorities in Applying Article 82 EC Treaty to Abusive Exclusionary Conduct by Dominant Undertakings. http://ec.europa.eu/competition/antitrust/art82/guidance.pdf

J Häckner (1999), 'Market Delineation and Product Differentiation,' http://wwwnesuse/paper/wp99_07pdf

J Hausman, 'A Proposed Method for Analysing Competition among Differentiated Products' [1992] Antitrust Law Journal 60, 889–900.

B Hawk, 'The American (Anti-Trust) Revolution: Lessons for the EEC?' [1988] ECLR 53.

Hinchliffe, 'When Is an Agreement Not an Agreement?' [2004] 5/6 Business Law Review 108.

H Hotelling, 'Stability in Competition' (1929) Economic Journal, 39, 41–57.

KN Hylton & M Salinger, Tying Law and Policy: A Decision—Theoretic Approach [2001] 69 Antitrust Law Journal 469.

E Iacobucci, 'Tying as Quality Control: A Legal and Economic Analysis', University of Toronto, Faculty of Law, Law and Economics Research Paper No 01-09, http://paperssrncom/abstract=293602.

ICN Unilateral Conduct Working Group for the 6th Annual Conference of the ICN in May 2007 in Moscow http://wwwinternationalcompetition-networkorg/media/library/unilateral_conduct/Objectives%20of%20Unilateral%20Conduct%20May%2007pdf

ICN Special Program for Kyoto Annual Conference Report on Abuse of Superior Bargaining Position, wwwinternationalcompetitionnetworkorg

International Competition Network (Seventh Annual Conference), Special Program on Abuse of Superior Bargaining Position, Germany response http://wwwicn-kyotoorg/documents/germanypdf

Immenga and Mestmäcker — Markert, Kommentar zum GWB, 1st edition 1981

A Irmen, JF Thisse, 'Competition in Multi-characteristics Spaces: Hotelling Was Almost Right' [1998] Journal of Economic Theory, 76–102.

A Jones and B Sufrin, 'EC Competition Law' (2nd edn, Oxford University Press, 2004).

A Jones, 'A Dominant Firm's Duty to Deal: EC and US Antitrust Law Compared' in Handbook of Research in Transatlantic Antitrust (Philip Marsden (ed), (British Institute of International and Comparative Law) 2006).

I Kokkoris, 'Antitrust Encyclopedia', French Report by Christophe Clarenc, wwwconcurrencescom

I Kokkoris, 'The Development of the concept of Collective Dominance in the European Community Merger Regulation From its Inception to its Current Status' [2007] World Competition, September.

I Kokkoris, *Competition Cases from the European Union* (Sweet and Maxwell, London, 2007).

S Kon, S Turnbull, 'Pricing and the dominant firm: implications of the Competition Commission Appeal Tribunal's judgment in the Napp case' [2007] 24(2) ECLR 70–86.

V Korah, *An Introductory Guide to EC Competition Law and Practice* (5th edn, OUP, 1994).

N Kroes, 'Preliminary Thoughts on Policy Review of Article 82' speech given on 23 September 2005 at the Fordham Corporate Law Institute New York http://europaeu/rapid/pressReleasesActiondo?reference=SPEECH/05/537&format=HTML&aged=0&language=EN&guiLanguage=en

N Kroes, 'European Competition Policy: Delivering Better Markets and Better Choices', 15 September 2005, available at http://europaeu/rapid/pressReleasesActiondo?reference=SPEECH/05/512&format=HTML&aged=0& language=EN&guiLanguage=en

K-U Kühn, R Stillman, C Caffarra (2005) 'Economic theories of bundling and their policy implications in abuse cases: an assessment in light of the Microsoft case' [2005] 1(1) Euro CJ 85–121.

K-U Kühn, R Stillman, C Caffarra, Economic Theories of Bundling and Their Policy Implication in Abuse Cases: An Assessment in Light of the Microsoft Case, CEPR Discussion Paper No 4756 (2005).

T Lampert, Evaluating Bundled Discounts, 89 Minn L Rev 1688 (2004–2005)

JT Lang, 'Defining Legitimate Competition: Companies' Duties to Supply Competitors and Access to Essential Facilities' [1994] 18 Fordham International Law Journal 437.

JT Lang, 'Defining Legitimate Competition: How to Clarify Pricing Abuses Under Article 82' [2002] FILJ 83.

JT Lang and R O'Donoghue, 'Defining Legitimate Competition: How to Clarify Pricing Abuses under Article 82EC' [2002] 26 Fordham International Law Journal 83.

JT Lang, 'European Competition Law and Compulsory Licensing of Intellectual Property Rights—a Comprehensive Principle' [2004] 4 Europarättslig Tidskrift 558–588.

JT Lang, 'Fundamental Issues Concerning Abuse Under Article 82 EC' [2005] Regulatory Policy Institute 19.

M Lao, 'Aspen Skiing and Trinko: Antitrust Intent and Sacrifice' [2005] 73 Antitrust Law Journal 171.

Law on Competition of 17 May 2004 (the '2004 Law') http://wwwlegiluxpubliclu/leg/a/archives/2004/0762605/0762605pdf?SID=9c660fa1e8e5446d8be91743b21d36cb#page=2

T Leary, 'The search for Consensus on the Revival of Section 5', FTC Workshop on Section 5, 17 October 2008, www.ftc.gov

J Leibowitz, 'Tales from the Crypt', FTC Workshop on Section 5, 17 October 2008, www.ftc.gov.

A Lindsay The EC Merger Regulation: Substantive Issues (Sweet & Maxwell, London, 2003).

M Lorenz, M Lübbig and A Russel, 'Price Discrimination, a Tender Story' [2005] ECLR 355.

L Luce Nollet, Y Utzschneider, 'France: Award of radio frequency licences not subject to jurisdiction of competition authority' [2002] 23(2) ECLR N26–27, France Telecom SA v Numericable SNC [2001] ECC 2.

MC Lucey (2006), 'Unforeseen consequences of Article 3 of EU Regulation 1/2003' [2006] 27(10) (ECLR) 558–563.

A Majumdar, 'The Role of A Consumer Harm Test in Competition Policy', Draft for Discussion (2007), http://64233169104/search?q=cache:7X1vk0Kcns4J: wwwlucedu/law/academics/special/center/antitrust/pdfs/consumer_harmpdf+differentiated+products+markets+in+competition+policy&hl=en&ct=clnk&cd=90&gl=us

J Malinauskaite, 'The development of "consumer welfare and its application in the competition law of the European Community and Lithuania' [2007] 18(10) ICCLR 354–364.

Market investigation references Guidance about the making of references under Part 4 of the Enterprise Act wwwoftgovuk

Market Investigation References: Competition Commission Guidelines, wwwcompetition-commissionorguk

Jedlickova B McCabe, 'Boundaries between unilateral and multilateral conducts in vertical restraints' [2008] 29(10) ECLR 600–607.

RP McAfee, J McMillan and MD Whinston, Multiproduct Monopoly, Commodity bundling and correlation of values [1989] 104 Q J Econ 371.

V Mertikopoulou, 'DG Competition's discussion paper on the application of Article 82 of the EC Treaty to exclusionary abuses: the proposed economic reform from a legal point of view' [2007] 28(4) ECLR 241–251.

Michael Salinger at the FTC Workshop on Section 5, 17 October 2008, www.ftc.gov.

G Monti, 'The Concept of Dominance in Article 82' [2006] European Competition Journal 31–52.

M Motta (2007), *Competition Policy* (Cambridge University Press, 2007)

M Mussa, S Rosen, 'Monopoly and Product Quality', [1978] 18 Journal of Economic Theory 301–317.

P Muysert, 'Price Discrimination—An Unreliable Indicator of Market Power' [2004] 6 ECLR 350.

Nalebuff, Bundling, Tying and Portfolio Effects, DTI Economics Paper No1, February 2003.

C Nagy, 'Refusal to deal and the doctrine of essential facilities in US and EC competition law: a comparative perspective and a proposal for a workable analytical framework' [2007] 32(5) EL Rev 664–685.

E Navarro Varona, 'Amendments to the Spanish Law for the Defence of Competition' [2000] 21(4) ECLR 235–238.

A Nevo, 'Mergers with Differentiated Products: The Case of Ready-to-Eat Cereal', Competition Policy Center Book CPC99-002 (1997) http://repositoriescdliborg/iber/cpc/CPC99-002

G Niels, H Jenkins, Reform of Article 82: Where the Link Between Dominance and Effects Breaks Down [2005] ECLR.

L Nollet, 'France: Anti-competitive Practices' [2003] 24(7) ECLR N116–117.

R O'Donoghue and J PadillaJ, *The Law and Economics of Article 82 EC* (OUP, Oxford, 2006); OECD 'The Essential Facilities Concept' Background Note, OCDE/GD(96)113.

OECD, 'Competition Policy Roundtable on Loyalty and Fidelity Discounts and Rebates' (4 March 2003) 1–239.

OECD, 'Competition Policy Roundtable on Predatory Foreclosure' (15 March 2005) 1–279.

P Oliver, 'The Concept of "Abuse" of a Dominant Position under Article 82 EC: Recent Developments in Relation to Pricing' [2006] 1(2) Euro CJ 315–339.

OECD brief, 'Substantial Market Power' http://wwwoecdorg/dataoecd/58/28/41257462pdf September 2008.

A Perrot, 'Towards an Effects-based Approach of Price Discrimination' in The Pros and Cons of Price Discrimination (Swedish Competition Authority, 2005).

D Price, 'Abuse of a dominant position—the tale of nails, milk cartons and TV guides' [1990] 11(2) ECLR 80–90.

Report by the EAGCP—'An Economic Approach to Article 82' http://eceuropaeu/comm/competition/antitrust/art82/indexhtml

D Ridyard, 'Exclusionary Pricing and Price Discrimination Abuses under Article 82—An Economic Analysis' [2002] 6 ECLR 286.

D Ridyard, 'Tying and Bundling—Cause for Complaint?' [2005] 26(6) ECLR 316–319.

G Robinson, 'On Refusing to Deal with Rivals' [2002] 87 Cornell Law Review 1177.

L Röller, 'Exploitative Abuses', in Ehlermann and Marquis (eds), *European Competition Law Annual 2007: A Reformed Approach to Article 82 EC* (Hart Publishing, Oxford, 2008).

T Rosch, Welcoming Remarks, FTC Workshop on Section 5, 17 October 2008, www.ftc.gov.

P Roth (2001), 'Bellamy and Child European Community Law of Competition' (5th edn, Sweet and Maxwell, London).

I Roudard (1989), 'The New French Legislation on Competition' [1989] ECLR 10(2) 205–232.

E Rousseva, 'The Concept of 'Objective Justification' of an Abuse of a Dominant Position: Can it help to Modernise the Analysis under Article 82 EC?' [2005] 2(2) Comp L Rev.

M Salinger, 'A Graphical Analysis of Bundling' [1995] 68 J Bus 85 .

R Schmalensee, 'Output and Welfare Implications of Monopolistic Third-Degree Price Discrimination' [1981] 71 The American Economic Review 242

R Schmalensee, Gaussian Demand and Commodity Bundling, [1984] 57 J Bus 211.

M Schödermeier, Metro II et les limites de la distribution sélective (Cahiers de droit européen, 1987).

M Schödermeier, 'Collective dominance revisited: an analysis of the EC Commission's new concepts of oligopoly control' [1990] 11(1) ECLR, 11(1) 28–34.

D Seidmann, 'Bundling as a Facilitating Device: A Reinterpretation of Leverage Theory [1991] 58 Economica 491.

A Shaked, J Sutton, 'Relaxing Price Competition through Product Differentiation' [1982] Review of Economic Studies 49.

C Shapiro, 'Mergers with Differentiated Products' [1996] Antitrust 10.

J Shaw, 'Inter versus intra brand competition: dominant positions and ancillary markets' [1987] E L Rev 12(3) 195–199.

N Singh and X Vives, 'Price and Quantity Competition in a Differentiated Duopoly' [1984] Rand Journal of Economics 15, 546–554.

M Sousa Ferro (2007) 'Reassessing Borders Between Agreements and Unilateral Practices after Case C-74/04', Volkswagen II' [2007] 28(3) ECLR 205–209.

D Spector, 'From harm to competitors to harm to competition: one more effort, please!' [2006] 2(1) Euro CJ 145–162.

C Stothers, 'Refusal to Supply as Abuse of a Dominant Position: Essential Facilities in the European Union' [2001] 7 ECLR.

C Stothers, 'Who Needs Intellectual Property? Competition Law and Restrictions on Parallel Trade Within the European Economic Area' [2005] 27 (12) EIPR 458–466.

A Stratakis, 'Comparative Analysis of the US and EU Approach and Enforecement of the Essential Facilities Doctrine' [2006] 27 ECLR 434.

J Tirole, *The Theory of Industrial Organization* (Cambridge, Mass, The MIT Press, 1988).

J Tirole, 'The Analysis of Tying Cases: A Primer' [2005] 1 Comp Policy Int'l 1.

G Triantafillakis in I Kokkoris, *Competition Cases from the European Union* (Sweet and Maxwell, London, 2007).

Y Utzschneider, 'France: Franchise Agreement—Positin of Economic Dependence' [1998] 19 (5) ECLR, N82.

HR Varian, 'Price Discrimination and Social Welfare' [1985] 75 The American Economic Review 870.

J Venit, 'Article 82: The Last Frontier—Fighting Fire with Fire?' [2005] 28 Fordham International Law Journal 1157.

Verordnung Gegen Missbrauch Wirtschaftlicher Machtstellungen, Reichsbesetzblatt [R6B1] I, 1067, 2 November 1923.

B Vesterdorf, 'Article 82 EC: Where do we stand after the Microsoft judgement?', http://wwwiccqmulacuk/GAR/Vesterdorfpdf

L Vogel (1998), 'Competition Law and Buying Power: the Case for a New Approach in Europe' [1998] 19 (1) ECLR 4–11.

G Werden, 'A Robust Test for Consumer Welfare Enhancing Mergers among Sellers of Differentiated Products' [1982] Journal of Industrial Economics 44, 409–414.

G Werden, L Froeb (2002), 'Calibrated Economic Models Add Focus, Accuracy, and Persuasiveness to Merger Analysis', www2owenvanderbiltedu/lukefroeb/papers/sca10pdf

R Whish (2003), *Competition Law* (5th edn, Butterworths, UK).

EC CASE LAW

Case 6/72 *Europemballage Corp and Continental Can Co. Inc v Commission* (Continental Can), [1973] ECR I-215.

British Airways plc v Commission, C95/04 P.

Oscar Bronner v Mediaprint C-7/97 [1998] ECR I-7791.

Case C-6/72 *Continental Can v Commission* [1973] ECR 215.

Microsoft [2007] OJ L 32/23, *Microsoft Corp v Commission*, T-201/04 R, [2004] ECR II-4463, *Microsoft Corp v Commission* T-201/04, 17/09/2007.

Case M308 *Kali und Salz/MdK/Treuhand* [1998] OJ C275/3;

Cases 68/94 and C-30/95 *France v Commission, Societe Commerciale es Potasses et de l'Azore (SCPA) v Commission* [1998] ECR I-1375.

Case 27/76, *United Brands Co. and United Brands Continental BV v Commission* [1978], ECR I-207.

Case 85/76, *Hoffmann-La Roche & Co AG v Commission* [1979] ECR I-461.

ABG (1977) OJ L117/1.

Magill (1989) OJ L78/43.

Wea-Filipacchi Music SA (72/480/CEE), [1972] O.J. L303/52.

Miller International Schallplatten GmbH (76/915/CEE), [1976] O.J. L357/40.

The Distillers Company Limited, Conditions of Sale and Price Terms (78/163/CEE), [1978] O.J. L50/16.

Johnson & Johnson (80/1283/CEE), [1980] O.J. L377/16.

Fisher-Price/Quaker Oats Ltd—Toyco (88/86/CEE), [1988] O.J. L49/19.

Konica (88/172/CEE), [1988] O.J. L78/34.C-22/78, *Hugin v European Commission* [1979] ECR I-1869.

Gøttrup-Klim e.a. Grovvareforeninger v Dansk Landbrugs Grovvareselskab AmbA, C-250/92 [1994] ECR I-5641.

BA/Virgin [2000] OJ L30/1.

Case M3216 *Oracle/PeopleSoft* [2005] OJ L218/6.

Case M3333 *Sony/BMG* [2005] OJ L62/30.

Case 322/81, *Michelin v Commission* [1983] ECR-3461.

Case T-229/94 *Deutsche Bahn v Commission* [1997] ECR II-1689.

Commission Decision 96/478 *Adalat* [1996] O.J. L201/1.

Case T-41/96 R *Bayer AG v Commission* [1996] E.C.R. II-381, [2000] E.C.R. II-3383.

Case C-62/86, *AKZO Chemie BV v Commission*, [1991] ECR I-3359.

Cases 6&7/73, *Instituto Chemioterapico Italiano SpA and Commercial Solvents Corp v Commission (Commercial Solvents)* [1974] ECR 223.

Case T-30/89, *Hilti v Commission* [1991], ECR II-1439, confirmed C-53/92P, [1994] ECR I-666.

Case T-51/89, *Tetra Pak Rausing SA v Commission (Tetra Pak I)* [1990] E.C.R. II-309, [1991] 4 C.M.L.R. 334.

Case T-83/91, *Tetra Pak Rausing SA v Commission (Tetra Pak II)*, [1994] ECR II-755.

Case T-111/96, *ITT Promedia NV v Commission (Promedia)*, [1998] ECR II-2937.

US CASE LAW

In the Matter of Negotiated Data Solutions LLC, FTC File No. 051 0094 (Jan. 23, 2008).

In the Matter of Valassis Communications, Inc No 51-0008 (Mar. 14, 2006).

FTC v. Ind. Fed'n of Dentists, 476 US 447, 454 (1986).

FTC v. Sperry & Hutchinson, 405 US 223, 239, 244 (1972).

FTC v. Brown Shoe Co., 384 US 316, 321 (1966).

US v. duPont, 351 US 377 (1956).

Federal Trade Commission v Motion Picture Advertising Service Co 344 US 392 (1953).

FTC v RF Keppel & Bros Inc 291 US 304, 310 (1934).

Ethyl, 729 F.2d.

Boise Cascade, 630 F.2d.